THE LIBRARY
ST. MARY'S COLLEGE OF MARYLAND
ST. MARY'S CITY, MARYLAND 20686

Southern Literary Studies
Louis D. Rubin, Jr., Editor

*Pastoral
in
Antebellum
Southern
Romance*

The Valley of Virginia and the Peaks of Otter

Pastoral
in
Antebellum
Southern
Romance

JAN BAKKER

LOUISIANA STATE UNIVERSITY PRESS

BATON ROUGE AND LONDON

Copyright © 1989 by
Louisiana State University Press
All rights reserved
Manufactured in the United States of America

First printing
98 97 96 95 94 93 92 91 90 89   5 4 3 2 1
Designer: Albert Crochet
Typeface: Linotron Aster
Typesetter: G & S Typesetters, Inc.
Printer & Binder: Thomson-Shore, Inc.

Library of Congress Cataloging-in-Publication Data

Bakker, Jan, 1936–
    Pastoral in antebellum Southern romance / Jan Bakker.
        p.   cm.
    Bibliography: p.
    Includes index.
    ISBN 0-8071-1531-2 (alk. paper)
    1. Pastoral fiction, American—Southern States—History and
criticism.   2. American fiction—19th century—History and
criticism.   3. Southern States—Intellectual life—19th century.
4. Southern States in literature.   5. Romanticism—Southern States.
I. Title.
PS261.B25   1989
813'.409'321734—dc20   89-32033
                                                                         CIP

Portions of Chapter 2 were originally published, in slightly different form,
as "Parallel Water Journeys into the American Eden in John Davis's *The
First Settlers of Virginia* and F. Scott Fitzgerald's *The Great Gatsby*," in *Early
American Literature*, XVI (Spring, 1981), 50–53. Portions of Chapter 3 were
originally published, in slightly different form, as "Some Other Versions of
Pastoral: The Disturbed Landscape in Tales of the Antebellum South," in *No
Fairer Land: Studies in Southern Literature Before 1900*, edited by J. Lasley
Dameron and James W. Mathews (Troy, N.Y., 1986), 67–86. Portions of Chap-
ter 4 are reprinted by permission of The University of Tennessee Press, from
"Time and Timelessness in Images of the Old South: Pastoral in John Pendleton Kennedy's *Swallow Barn* and *Horse-Shoe Robinson*," in *Tennessee Studies
in Literature XXVI*, edited by Allison R. Ensor and Thomas J. A. Heffernan.
Copyright © 1981 by The University of Tennessee Press. Portions of Chapter 6
were originally published, in slightly different form, as "'. . . a confusing and
sterile fulfillment': The Pastoral Pessimism of William Gilmore Simms," in
Encyclia, LV (1978), 132–41, and in *The Rectangle*, LVIII (Spring, 1983),
45–53; and as "The Pastoral Pessimism of William Gilmore Simms," in *Studies in American Fiction*, XI (Spring, 1983), 81–90.

Frontispiece, from Volume I of *Picturesque America; or, The Land We Live In*,
edited by William Cullen Bryant (New York, 1872), courtesy Special Collections, University of Tennessee.

The paper in this book meets the guidelines for permanence and durability of
the Committee on Production Guidelines for Book Longevity of the Council
on Library Resources. ⊗

For my mother
Elise Anna Wilhelmena

and in memory of my father
Albertus Haaie

The beginning of autumn;
What is the fortune teller
Looking so surprised at?
—Buson

Contents

Acknowledgments

Grants of funds and release time from the University of Tennessee at Knoxville and Utah State University aided me during the initiation and conclusion of work on this study. I am especially grateful to Utah State for a year's sabbatical leave in 1985–86. John Dobson and Nick Wyman of the Special Collections Library at the University of Tennessee were always helpful and congenial as I was doing my research and writing. Staff at the Rare Book Department of the Alderman Library at the University of Virginia were helpful in their turn as well, particularly Mildred K. Abraham, who responded so readily to a recent request I made. Kay Newton and Charlotte Wright read stages of the manuscript along the way. I am thankful to them for their suggestions, as I am to the readers and editors of Louisiana State University Press, and to the late Richard Beale Davis, mentor and friend.

*Pastoral
in
Antebellum
Southern
Romance*

Introduction

In antebellum pastoral the idyll is not the thing. What lies behind it is. In the outdoor, largely adventure romances of such
authors of the Old South as John Davis, Isaac Holmes, Henry
Ruffner, James Kirke Paulding, John Pendleton Kennedy,
William Alexander Caruthers, William Gilmore Simms, and
John Esten Cooke, images of a rural ideal serve as a commentary upon the actual world. This imagery is sometimes routine, sometimes startling, and sometimes profound. It is significantly consistent in their now extravagant, now mellow
fictions of exploration, courtship, and derring-do in the forests of a doomed frontier; their stories of bravery, danger, and
love in brutal, disruptive Revolutionary or Indian warfare;
their tales of bucolic life and love on threatened farms or
plantations.

Because the strength of pastoral imagery lies in its power of
suggestion, I find that its use gives to the work of the male romancers of the Old South the quality that Richard Chase believes is so important in American fiction: the refusal of the
explicit for the sake of setting up a double meaning. Southern
pastoral juxtaposes a real, changing world with an idyllic,
static vision. In the works I will consider, this contrast creates
a surprising dichotomy that reveals the other side, the duality of human experiences and dreams. This is the quality,
Chase further states, that makes a genuine, enduring fiction.
Antebellum southern idyll is typical, too—in the words of
Renato Poggioli in his definitive studies of pastoral in *The
Oaten Flute*—of modern or inverted pastoral, which is ironic
and ambiguous, evoking a bucolic aspiration only to deny

it.[1] Sometimes this pastoral denial or inversion even evokes a shudder.

A similar pattern of imagery, incidentally, does *not* occur in the fiction produced by the many female writers of the antebellum South who were among that "damned mob of scribbling women" Nathaniel Hawthorne dismissed with annoyance. Such southern authors as Caroline Howard Gilman, Caroline Lee Hentz, Augusta Jane Evans Wilson, Mary Jane Holmes, and Eliza Ann Dupuy, to name a handful, wrote indoor, triumph-of-love romances typical of the female literary domestics of the time whom Mary Kelley discusses in *Private Woman, Public Stage*. The tales of the women writers of the Old South are material for another study at another time.

For explorers like Arthur Barlowe and Walter Raleigh, who were among its first white observers, the southern landscape recalled the *locus amoenus*, or pleasant place, of traditional pastoral literature. This illusion, this dream of the land, persisted in the developing mythos of the South. There, in the nineteenth century, town life took a second place to country life as an ideal existence. The businessman, lawyer, physician, or writer of Charleston or Savannah, for instance, hoped to make his fortune in the city and then retire to a bucolic, self-sustaining plantation. In the South, W. J. Cash writes, the old frontier pattern of rugged outdoor activity remained a valued way of life well into the twentieth century.[2] It was from looking for themes in their own land that perceptive nondomestic antebellum southern romancers derived their complex pastoral images. On one level, their pastoral juxtapositions foreshadow the idealism of *I'll Take My Stand*, whose essays, written in the 1920s, create an overall picture of a peaceful, hardworking, civilized agricultural society in the South.[3]

On another, and more arresting, level, antebellum southern

1. Richard Chase, *The American Novel and Its Tradition* (New York, 1957), viii–ix; Renato Poggioli, *The Oaten Flute* (Cambridge, Mass., 1975), 34.
2. W. J. Cash, *The Mind of the South* (New York, 1954), 106.
3. *I'll Take My Stand: The South and the Agrarian Tradition*, by Twelve Southerners (New York, 1962), *passim*.

pastoral shows not so much a world in bucolic tranquility and security as a world that is threatened by busy and destructive social, economic, and political fluctuations. This play of imagery can be seen in the earliest southern romance of all, John Davis's *The First Settlers of Virginia*, as well as in the last of the antebellum romances, written by William Gilmore Simms and John Esten Cooke. The consistency of the pessimistic theme that attaches to antebellum pastoral marks the inception of that "fundamental image" Alfred Kazin discerns in William Faulkner's fiction—to name but one recent southern author in whose work this idea can be found—of "life as a perpetual breaking down."[4] In their handling of pastoral allusion and incident, Davis, Kennedy, Simms, Cooke, and other antebellum southern writers show an acute awareness of the architectonics of an important literary form linked to a tradition going all the way back to the georgics of Theocritus and Virgil. In their pastoral aesthetic, authors of the Old South display not only their creative, descriptive abilities, but also their concern about the immediate problems of their nation and section. However subtly they express themselves, they do indeed show worry about the discomforting and alarming changes that were overwhelming their America—those inevitable incursions of history and time that gave them, as increasingly isolated southerners, a feeling of despair, of a losing battle, of familiar things and ways falling apart into an imminent doom.

Actually, perfect felicity is not reflected very deeply in serious pastoral; complacency is not the feeling it calls up in the thoughtful reader. Still, pastoral imagery can trick cursory readers by lulling them into accepting its picturesque bucolic nostalgia on face value alone. In reality, however, idyllic passages, references, and yearnings in romances of the Old South are deeply tinged with tragedy. The essential underlying theme in such tales is the loss of a sylvan American paradise. This theme neatly ties into what Northrop Frye has described

4. Alfred Kazin, *An American Procession: The Major American Writers from 1830 to 1930—The Crucial Century* (New York, 1984), 349.

as the perpetual, systematic re-creation in national litera-
tures of fundamental myths and archetypes.[5] On its most arresting level, then, pastoral imagery in certain antebellum
southern romances constitutes a mythic representation of human experience on the model of the biblical Fall and expul-
sion from Eden. This tragic theme of the disjunction of the
ideal and the real in American experience is tightly woven
into pastoral in the South's most significant fiction, from
Kennedy and Simms to Thomas Nelson Page, Ellen Glasgow,
Flannery O'Connor, and, of course, William Faulkner. It is
found also in the novels of withdrawal, blight, and acceptance of Walker Percy and James Dickey. In the final analysis,
pastoral allusion gives romances of the Old South a sym-
bolism and a realism that make them something more than
the merely regional expressions, as they so often have been
called, of the plantation ideal or of heroic, imaginary frontier
or Revolutionary War deeds.

A very serious, almost allegorical quality infuses antebellum
pastoral with a dialectic force whose contrasts of dream and
reality work to compromise or question the pastoral's recurring images of a southern *locus amoenus*. This dialectic of
opposites creates the tension that Michael Squires in *The
Pastoral Novel* says vitalizes fiction that relies heavily on pastoral imagery for structure and theme.[6]

It is not my intention to place certain antebellum southern
romances on a level with the pastoral novels of George Eliot,
Thomas Hardy, and D. H. Lawrence that Squires discusses.
Rather, I want to show how elements of pastoral work as
a form within the form of adventure romances and outdoor
tales of the Old South to give this body of American fiction a
greater aesthetic beauty, as literature, and more historical
importance, as social criticism, than many readers and commentators so far have acknowledged. Through pastoral allusion, such works confront contemporary problems in southern and national society in America; hence, they rise above

5. Northrop Frye, *Anatomy of Criticism: Four Essays* (Princeton, 1957),
188–200.
6. Michael Squires, *The Pastoral Novel: Studies in George Eliot, Thomas
Hardy, and D. H. Lawrence* (Charlottesville, 1974), 25.

the superficiality that Hinton R. Helper in the 1860s, and Louis D. Rubin, Jr., and Lucinda H. MacKethan in the 1970s and 1980s, say mars the creative writing of the antebellum South.⁷ Here I carry MacKethan's study of the dream of Arcady in postbellum and twentieth-century southern literature back to its neglected roots.

7. Hinton R. Helper, *The Impending Crisis of the South: How to Meet It* (New York, 1860), 400, 402, 409; Louis D. Rubin, Jr., *William Elliott Shoots a Bear: Essays on the Southern Literary Imagination* (Baton Rouge, 1975), 27; Louis D. Rubin, Jr., *The Writer in the South* (Athens, Ga., 1972), 30; Louis D. Rubin, Jr., *et al.* (eds.), *The History of Southern Literature* (Baton Rouge, 1985), 11, 92, 165, 174; Lucinda Hardwick MacKethan, *The Dream of Arcady: Place and Time in Southern Literature* (Baton Rouge, 1980), 210.

1

An Approach to
Antebellum Pastoral

Already in the earliest promotional writings about the South, there is evidence of a peculiar pastoral tension, of counterbalances or dichotomies within idyllic imagery of the kind that would become such an important aesthetic and critical device in antebellum southern romances. "Felicity teeming *Virginia*," Edward Williams called it, these "sun-drenched climates."[1] Writers such as Williams saw the southern New World in terms of traditional European pastoral imagery and its *locus amoenus*. This is always pictured as a beautifully cultivated rural place of sunny green repose and contemplation. Birds sing in the groves there, streams and fountains are sparkling, clear, and musical, while flocks graze and play and low, and summer-idle shepherds and shepherdesses yearn, court—but rarely marry—and gambol to melodies of panpipes in shady, grassy places. The pleasant country spot is circumscribed, however, by an outside world beyond the comforting trees and hills. This is a world whose ways and inhabitants invariably pose a threat to the pastoral place to which they sometimes come for refuge, reorientation, and spiritual and physical refreshment among its orchards, meadows, and shade-dappled lanes. But these sojourners, these visitors, must leave again for their own world, frequently after having left some kind of trouble behind them. The *locus amoenus* is only a temporary place for outsiders, only a transitory experience.

1. Peter Force (ed.), *Tracts and Other Papers, Relating Principally to the Origin, Settlement, and Progress of the Colonies in North America* (4 vols.; New York, 1947), Vol. III, Sec. xi, p. 19.

About the time of Edward Williams's experience in Virginia, a fashionable Londoner and royal chaplain, Reverend Daniel Price, coined the phrase "the Garden of the world" in 1609 to describe a South he had only read about. Sir Walter Raleigh claimed that Paradise had been created in the same latitude as Virginia, "thirty-five degrees from the Equinoctial, and fifty-five from the North-pole, in a temperate Climate, full of excellent fruites." In Raleigh's arcadian new environment there was nothing of William Bradford's wintry New England with its "hideous and desolate wilderness full of wild beasts and wild men." For the enthusiastic Arthur Barlowe, the aromatic Virginia shore was reminiscent of the toil-free abundance of life as he understood it "in the first creation." The American natives, he also wrote, were "most gentle, loving, and faithfull, void of all guile, and treason, and such as lived after the manner of the golden age." [2]

But from the beginning, many such edenic descriptions of the New World betray a strange dichotomy, a pause that reveals the writers' puzzled, pained awareness of a conflict between southern dream and southern reality. Before John Smith left Jamestown, he was both optimistic and worried. Virginia would possess the best farm land in the world, he reflected, were it fully and properly cultivated and "inhabited by industrious people." Then he paused, fearful of failure for the new Eden off the James River because of the laziness of the settlers. Sure enough, when William Strachey arrived at Jamestown in 1609 he discovered ruin. Surviving settlers crawled out of filthy hovels to greet him. His anger turned on these survivors, whose "sloth, riot, and vanity," he wrote, had caused such a sad state of affairs in the once hopeful colony. Their poverty came from idleness in a fruitful land. He had no pleasant thoughts either about noble savages. The Indians, he

2. Louis B. Wright, *The Colonial Search for a Southern Eden* (University, Ala., 1953), 28; Clarence W. Alvord and Lee Bidgood (eds.), *The First Explorations of the Trans-Allegheny Region by the Virginians, 1650–1674* (Cleveland, 1912), 112–13; William Bradford, *Of Plymouth Plantation, 1620–1647*, ed. Samuel Eliot Morison (New York, 1952), 62; David Beers Quinn (ed.), *The Roanoke Voyages, 1584–1590* (London, 1955), Ser. II, Vol. CIV, pp. 93–94, 108; Louis B. Wright (ed.), *A Voyage to Virginia in 1609: Two Narratives* (Charlottesville, 1964), 60.

felt, were crafty and untrustworthy despite their stoicism and physical beauty.[3]

A particularly saddened anonymous commentator looked at the Virginia settlement in 1610. His words point directly to the conflict or tension of dream versus reality, posited later by pastoral allusion in southern fiction. Musing over the failure of the bickering colonists to take advantage of the land's quiet richness, he wrote soberly: "It is but a golden slumber, that dreameth of any humane felicity, which is not sauced with some contingent misery."[4]

Early in the eighteenth century, Robert Beverley observed the second Fall in the American garden most pointedly of all, and with appealing whimsy. "I am an Indian," he writes, as he sets out in "plain dress" to guide the reader through Virginia's history and forested lands. His *History and Present State of Virginia* of 1705 is the first account written by a native of the colony. After routinely comparing the lushness of Virginia to Paradise, he wonders—as William Bartram does on his travels later in the century—about the ruined farmlands and woodlands he sees all over his otherwise bucolic South. Ironically, Beverley observes that it was the very "Liberality of Nature" upon which the colonists sponged that had corrupted them into the "slothful Indolence" that ruined their morale and the bounty of the earth itself. He wonders how such a strange turnabout from promising beginnings could have happened. He ends his history wistfully, hoping his thoughts will arouse his countrymen after all to "make the most of all those happy Advantages which nature has given them."[5] Still, in the conclusion of Beverley's story of a compromised Virginia idyll there lingers that note of criticism and loss inherent in all pastoral description.

The possibilities of a literal application of the classical bucolic dream of southern arcadia were perceived by Thomas

---

3. John Lankford (ed.), *Captain John Smith's America* (New York, 1967), 4, 17; Wright (ed.), *A Voyage to Virginia*, 63–67.

4. Force (ed.), *Tracts and Other Papers*, Vol. III, Sec. i, p. 24.

5. Robert Beverley, *The History and Present State of Virginia*, ed. Louis B. Wright (Chapel Hill, 1947), 9, 16, 233, 314, 319; William Bartram, *Travels Through North and South Carolina, Georgia, East and West Florida*, ed. Mark Van Doren (New York, 1928), 102, 199.

Jefferson in his vision of an industry-shunning American middle ground of self-sustaining farmers and craftsmen and small towns. This was his reverie at his own rural retreat, Monticello. His middle ground was a *via media* between Old World decadence and New World wilderness; a golden mean between palace and forest created in well-maintained domains of democratic and virtuous farmers and husbandmen. These were the "chosen people of God," he wrote in his one published book, *Notes on the State of Virginia* (1784); they were the stable bulwark of the nation against the "casualties and caprice" of trade and the "mobs of great cities." In a more down-to-earth mood, however, he stated in a subsequent letter of 1785 that his ideal for America was impossible from political and practical standpoints. Jefferson ruefully admitted that his countrymen were just too fond of navigation and commerce for his ideal to be in the end anything more than a passing reflection.[6]

The formula of pastoral imagery in pre-nineteenth-century writing about the South depicts a fallen garden, and muses upon humankind's lost estate. Those who came to the New World's Eden did not find peace or revitalization in it after all. They brought their own disharmonies with them, the whole teeming, disappointing European world from which they had sought to flee. What evolves in early tracts, histories, and later fictions about the nascent South is an apposite and subtle commentary upon the fallacy of humanity's age-old and hopeless dream of reacquiring somehow, somewhere, someday an idyllic, tranquil earthly Eden.

The strength of pastoral as a literary device lies in its power of suggestion and its recollection of humanity's great loss. What seems on the surface to be an imagery of escapism really provides no way out for the reader at all. An archetypal story emerges from the descriptive and promotional writings by observers of the pre-nineteenth-century South as they look with awe on a naturally bucolic and fruitful landscape that

6. Thomas Jefferson, *Notes on the State of Virginia*, ed. William Peden (Chapel Hill, 1955), 164–65; Thomas Jefferson, *The Writings of Thomas Jefferson*, ed. Andrew Lipscomb (20 vols.; Washington, D.C., 1903), V,183–84, VI,277, X,356, 431.

has been marred before their very eyes. So a peculiar duality in their perception of the sojourner, or settler, and the garden, or nature, in America exists even in the earliest commentators' seemingly facile writings. As a result, these writers attain in their own right an element of that particular setting, or machinery, as William Empson refers to it in his study of pastoral, for "imposing" the "social and metaphysical ideas on which pastoral depends." After all, pastoral characteristically deals with the complexities of life against a background of apparent simplicity.[7]

As, in their turn, generally overlooked antebellum southern writers investigate the meaning of human experience in a fallen world, they depict a spoiled pastoral that places them in the literary mainstream, along with such better-known and often studied contemporaries as James Fenimore Cooper, Henry David Thoreau, Nathaniel Hawthorne, and Herman Melville. Antebellum pastoral is a distinct phase in the development of what Charles L. Sanford in *The Quest for Paradise* calls the main theme in twentieth-century American literature: the "dispossession from paradise." He associates this with the nation's hurried industrialization and rapacious mercantile ethic.[8] In his way, William Gilmore Simms of South Carolina, the most widely read of the authors of the Old South, reflected on such issues with deeply troubled concern as well.

Although Theocritus is credited by a recent translator, Barriss Mills, with having invented the pastoral form in western literature, it was Virgil who developed the allegorical element in it, according to J. E. Congleton.[9] That is, Virgil developed in pastoral a mechanism, to use Empson's term, whereby a writer could criticize his time and place without appearing to do so, by depicting apparently contented people in an idyllic

---

7. William Empson, *Some Versions of Pastoral* (Hammondsworth, 1966), 25, 31, 34.

8. Charles L. Sanford, *The Quest for Paradise: Europe and the American Moral Imagination* (Urbana, Ill., 1961), 255.

9. Theocritus, *The Idylls of Theokritus*, trans. Barriss Mills (West Lafayette, Ind., 1963), vii; J. E. Congleton, *Theories of Pastoral Poetry in England, 1684–1798* (Gainesville, 1952), 5.

environment—a device that can delude the cursory or unre-
sponsive reader into thinking the author merely is being fan-
ciful or diverting.

Pastoral, Andrew V. Ettin writes in the latest full-length
study of the form, can speak with a "double voice . . . carrying
on two discussions simultaneously on different levels of significance." It provides a way "to unfold great matter of argument covertly," as "E. K." said much earlier in his Epistle
to Edmund Spenser's *Shepheards Calender.*[10] True, Tityrus in
Virgil's First Eclogue has found his rural repose. He is able to
keep it, however, only because he has connections among
politicians "outside," in Rome, who otherwise are taking
property away from old, established landholders to give in
reward to returning soldiers. Meliboeus, his neighbor who
has no connections, has lost his farm and sadly has to move
away. Rome here represents that traditional pastoral counterbalance or counterforce, the peripheral danger that invariably threatens the *locus amoenus.* How long, indeed, will
Tityrus himself be safe? Virgil's Rome in the First Eclogue recalls Jefferson's image of the cankerous city juxtaposed with
an image of the peaceful American agrarian landscape, and
dangerously encroaching upon it.[11]

Its allegorical intent, then, gives pastoral a special, subtle
dialectic force. As Leo Marx phrases it in his study of the usual
nineteenth-century New England writers, *The Machine in the
Garden*, pastoral in the literature of Thoreau, Hawthorne, and
Melville manages "to qualify, or call into question, or bring
irony to bear against the illusion of peace and harmony in a
green pasture. . . . The design brings a world which is more
'real' into juxtaposition with an idyllic vision."[12] These words
certainly apply as well to southern authors of the same period. In antebellum southern pastoral there is an unrelenting
flow of local images and actions that also symbolize this

10. Andrew V. Ettin, *Literature and the Pastoral* (New Haven, 1984), 113–14;
Edmund Spenser, *The Complete Poetical Works*, ed. R. E. Neil Dodge (Boston,
1936), 6.
11. Virgil, *The Works of Virgil*, trans. John Dryden (London, 1961), 3–6;
Jefferson, *Notes on the State of Virginia*, 165.
12. Leo Marx, *The Machine in the Garden: Technology and the Pastoral Ideal
in America* (New York, 1964), 25.

"real," disharmonious counterforce in human life moving through the trappings of bucolic idealization and romantic exaggeration.

In one instance, this pastoral counterforce is symbolized by the destructive "whirlwind axe" James Kirke Paulding hears cutting away at the peaceful, doomed forests he describes in *Letters from the South*. It is also seen in the dark, diseased, and smoking Jeffersonian cities of William Alexander Caruthers's *Kentuckian in New York*. The counterforce is significantly evident *inside* his southern garden in the danger posed by the aloof and incendiary slaves of the South Carolina plantation Belville. For John Esten Cooke the real, threatening world outside the rural retreat intrudes in a surprising image of townspeople literally frozen in midaction by the compelling train whistle that regularly pierces the peaceful air of bucolic Martinsburg in *Leather Stocking and Silk*. This event in Cooke's work is identical to something that disturbed Hawthorne's pastoral reverie in Sleepy Hollow, recounted in his *American Notebooks*, when "the long [train-whistle] shriek, harsh above all other harshness" suddenly brought "the noisy world into the midst of our slumbrous peace."[13]

For William Gilmore Simms, reality slips unexpectedly into a Revolutionary War idyll of camp life. Pontificating as usual, Lieutenant Porgy of *The Forayers* makes an uncharacteristic call for action: "Stagnation," he says to his dozing, well-fed companions. "Stagnation . . . is death." We need storms to agitate and to restore our equilibrium.[14] The *locus amoenus* Simms evokes with longing so often in landscape and plantation images, on the other hand, is an impossibly static place. On the contrary, Porgy insists here, humanity must be active and doing things—planting, industrializing, developing the land.

Simms himself had trouble in adjusting to this Yankee im-

13. James Kirke Paulding, *Letters from the South* (2 vols.; New York, 1835), I,71–72; William Alexander Caruthers, *The Kentuckian in New York; or, The Adventures of Three Southerners* (2 vols.; 1834; rpr. Ridgewood, N.J., 1968), I,33, II,66–67; John Esten Cooke, *Leather Stocking and Silk; or, Hunter John Myers and His Times* (New York, 1854), 8, 244; Nathaniel Hawthorne, *The American Notebooks*, ed. Randall Stewart (New Haven, 1933), 104.

14. William Gilmore Simms, *The Forayers; or, The Raid of the Dog-Days* (New York, 1855), 529.

age of America. Like the other intellectuals of the Old South whom Drew Gilpin Faust describes in *A Sacred Circle*, he had difficulty trying to reconcile the thoughtful and the active life, "to make the ideal actually relevant." Such reflective southerners developed a conviction that the civic values and ideals of the Revolutionary generation had been eroded by a half-century of Jacksonian democratic change and territorial expansion. So they grasped for symbols of stability and order to offset their feelings of drift and uncertainty, William R. Taylor says in *Cavalier and Yankee*, to quiet their uneasiness about iniquities and problems in their own society. Their versions of pastoral look toward that "essentially secular, latently political" quality that Leo Marx sees emerging in pastoralism of our own late twentieth century in America.[15]

In *Woodcraft*, Porgy is seen in an opposite vein from that in *The Forayers*. He makes his pastoral retreat to his restored and self-sustaining South Carolina plantation, that great symbol in the Old South of stability, order, and success. Porgy retires to bachelor indolence with a preference now for doing nothing at all. Others cultivate his lands for him. Pastoral shepherds appear never to have to work. In his futile, although wish-fulfilling, Porgy persona, Simms seems to be reacting to the unbucolic restlessness in the America of his time—the industrialization and immigration in the North; the agrarian expansionism of southerners to the southwest, leaving the land-wrecked, aristocratic Tidewater region to create a parvenu cotton culture in Mississippi and Alabama; and the nation-splitting agitation of the Abolitionist spirit, brought to one of its peaks by the publication of *Uncle Tom's Cabin* in 1852. But all the troubles remain out there seething nonetheless, pressing in on the softly green, pastoral spaces of Porgy's imaginary retreat at Glen-Eberley and Simms's real-life plantation, Woodlands, near Charleston—later burned to the ground by stragglers from Sherman's army.

15. Drew Gilpin Faust, *A Sacred Circle: The Dilemma of the Intellectual in the Old South, 1840–1860* (Baltimore, 1977), 59; William R. Taylor, *Cavalier and Yankee: The Old South and American National Character* (New York, 1961), 146–47, 322; Leo Marx, "Pastoralism in America," in Sacvan Bercovitch and Myra Jehlen (eds.), *Ideology and Classic American Literature* (New York, 1986), 68n14.

2

John Davis and the Southern Garden

At the turn of the eighteenth century, the young and ebullient Englishman John Davis toured and taught in the United States, mostly in the South, whose natural beauties and mild climate he enjoyed particularly. Jay B. Hubbell claims him "almost" as the first southern novelist. Indeed, Davis was the first writer who openly set out to fictionalize Virginia, whatever the stretches of truth might have been in the earliest promotional accounts of the area. Descriptions in his *First Settlers of Virginia* (1805) evoke the familiar garden imagery of explorers like Williams and Raleigh. Another of them, George Percy, also wrote in the pastoral mode to describe the untouched southern countryside he saw, whose "fair meadows and goodly tall trees" reminded him of a cultivated English "garden or Orchard." Davis's own imagined first settlers see the Virginia shore rising from the horizon "like a new creation from the sea,"[1] recalling the Garden of Eden and all that it implies. Whether or not a reader agrees with Hubbell's claim, it is in Davis's American romance that the thread of pastoral imagery is first woven into the fabric of the belletristic writing of the nineteenth-century South.

The simple plot of *First Settlers* follows John Smith from his optimistic arrival at Jamestown to his disgusted departure

---

1. Jay B. Hubbell, *The South in American Literature, 1607–1900* (Durham, 1954), 196; Louis B. Wright, *The Elizabethans' America* (London, 1965), 149 n1 (Percy quotation), 163, 167–71; John Davis, *The First Settlers of Virginia: An Historical Novel Exhibiting a View of the Rise and Progress of the Colony at James Town, a Picture of Indian Manners, the Countenance of the Country, and Its Natural Productions* (New York, 1806), 16. All references to the work will be taken from this edition and noted parenthetically by page number in the text.

from the colony. The story ends with the ominous inland cruise of Captain Argall, foreshadowing the corruption of the Indians and their dispossession from Eden while discontented white men waste the land. Of course, Davis retells the story of Smith's rescue by Pocahontas from Powhatan's executioner, Pocahontas's marriage to John Rolfe, and her death in England. He is more interested, though, in creating loving, lingering descriptions of the Virginia forests as he feels they must have been—with their strawberry fields, deer herds, and mockingbirds—than in describing the historical adventures of the Englishmen who first came there. The destructive activities of these people in nature's garden, however, provide his romance with its historical verisimilitude and with a pattern of irony and dilemma for subsequent questioning southern writers to follow.

As the sojourners who have come to stay, and so to wreck the *locus amoenus,* the settlers in the story provide the pastoral device of the counterforce that threatens the idyllic place. Their inevitable presence provides the element of ironic revelation that is the trick of serious pastoral. In the case of *First Settlers* and other nineteenth-century southern romances, this irony questions what both Leo Marx and R. W. B. Lewis have referred to as the American myth of a new beginning.[2] In drawing romantic parallels between Eden and Adam, and Virginia and Smith, Davis's intention is to show how humanity's second chance in the New World was lost all over again as quickly and certainly as in Genesis. Thus the formula of literary pastoral, whether American or classical, is complex under its guise of simplicity and provides the writer with a means for honest reflection on the dreams and contradictions of life. The apparent pastoral ideal of rural contentment is not at all to be taken as an obtainable one, but rather as the informative ideal Albert R. Cirillo describes, which actually posits the bitter plight of humankind since the Fall. For all the surface of romantic diversion in their adventure and outdoor tales, the most significant antebellum southern authors from

2. Marx, *The Machine in the Garden,* 228; R. W. B. Lewis, *The American Adam: Innocence, Tragedy, and Tradition in the Nineteenth Century* (Chicago, 1955), 5.

Davis on show an awareness of the disjunction between dream and reality in human experience. This consciousness clearly reflects what C. L. Sanford has termed the American tragic vision of life.[3]

The Indians in *First Settlers* have no idea what is in store for them as with awe and surprise they watch Captain Smith's ships enter the Chesapeake Bay: "The shores were now lined with the natives, who gazed with ineffable astonishment at the squadron under sail, and prostrated themselves at the thunder of their cannon. Their wonder may be conceived at the sight of a ship. They were scared out of their wits, to see the monster come sailing into their harbor, and spitting fire with a mighty noise out of her floating side" (18). Except for the attention Davis gives to the smoking Renaissance cannon, certainly a significant image in itself, there is no memorable detail in this description. It is a routine piece of writing. What, after all, did the startled Indians look like, or the sun on the water, or how did Smith's smelly, sea-worn ships appear approaching those sweetly aromatic shores? Where is the feeling here? The ships are appropriately likened to monsters, true, but the image is unsatisfactorily glib. The tone of the passage is "simple and flat," to use in another context E. M. Forster's phrase about a kind of characterization in fiction.[4] (In proper context, this phrase also applies to Davis's protagonists and those created by succeeding antebellum romancers.) This flat tone that Davis uses to describe historical events in his story is an important element of the pastoral aesthetic in *First Settlers*.

Davis pictures real occurrences in a spare, journalistic prose. In another instance, he uses a perfunctory list of adjectives—"profligate," "desperate," "dissipated" (157)—to describe the degeneration of the first settlers and their settlement. Readers are left to fill in the pictorial details for themselves. On the other hand, he describes with an appealing lyrical effulgence the surrounding forests and natural mead-

---

3. Albert R. Cirillo, "*As You Like It*: Pastoralism Gone Awry," *Journal of English Literary History*, XXXVIII (1971), 22, 38; Sanford, *The Quest for Paradise*, 28.
    4. E. M. Forster, *Aspects of the Novel* (New York, 1927), 77–78.

ows where the noble savages live. In this significant counter-
point of descriptive technique, Davis consciously juxtaposes a
curt, hard style with a dreamy, soft one. To give another example, the understandable fear the settlers experience at first
in the primeval forest is handled brusquely in undeveloped,
distant images of the "screams" of an eagle and the "roar" of
a cataract. At first these are the only sounds they hear that
punctuate the oppressiveness of Virginia's unfamiliar "regions of awful silence" (20). Again, the unsatisfactory brevity
with which Davis describes Smith's rescue by Pocahontas reduces the romantic adventure related by Smith to little more
than a passing reference (40).

After Smith has been saved by Pocahontas and released
by Powhatan, Nantaquas, Pocahontas's brother—and a fine
specimen of an Indian, as Davis describes him in his native
buckskins and proud bearing—guides the captain and his
troop back to Jamestown. There is no historical record of this
trip, in Smith's words or another's; however, it is here in
his fiction, in his dream of the lost Virginia forest, that Davis
indulges in the lyrical excess of nature description, which
obviously gave him a great deal of pleasure to write down.
He pastoralizes Virginia's untamed flora and fauna as the
white men move away from previous dangers into a comfort-
ing landscape of quietly grazing animals and sun-glistening
flowers and fields. This picturesque interlude recalls the cultivated appearance of a country house park, the very idea that
George Percy had in mind when he wrote his firsthand description of the same area. Davis in his turn writes: "Their
road lay through a country well stocked with oaks, poplars,
pines, cedars, and cypress. The theater of nature could be
scarcely more magnificent. For here rose tall forests, there
rolled a large river, and herds of wild animals were seen
browsing on its banks. The whole country displayed an exu-
berant verdure; the dogwood was shedding its blossoms in
the wilderness and the wild strawberry purpled the woods,
the fields, the plains" (52). Geese fly overhead while a mockingbird sings in a whitethorn, where Davis's focus and Smith's
attention come to rest. The songbird's melody, "melting into
the softest strains" (96), accompanies the travelers on their

way and recurs to evoke peace and harmony throughout the romance. It replaces the terrifying cry of the eagle. Mocking-birds and whippoorwills provide a musical background for idyllic interludes in *First Settlers*, lulling the colonists from their awareness of the real threats in the forest and the troubles in the settlement.

Tuneful animal or human sounds have always been part of a traditional pastoral landscape. So has been the shepherd. In antebellum southern romance this shepherd is transformed into the figure of the frontiersman-guide, a version of Cooper's Natty Bumppo, and Davis's John Smith is his prototype. Even Paulding in his *Letters from the South* pictures Smith as the archetypal resourceful, generous American woodsman. The typical, romanticized antebellum frontiersman, Smith has an innate sense of propriety and even gentleness under his rough soldier's exterior. He is a practical man, a shepherd-guide of others into the natural garden, like that bucolic herdsman of pastoral literature whom Leo Marx characterizes as an "efficacious mediator between the realm of organized society and the realm of nature."[5] Unlike the traditional pastoral shepherd, however, Smith is capable of calculated violence. He leads the first of the white men's depredations against the Indians when he mercilessly carries "terror through the country" (150) to prevent the natives from attacking Jamestown. True to form, Davis does not devote much time or detail to this adventure. Smith is strong and graceful, and his eye is ready "to command, to threaten, to soothe" (37). At work in Jamestown, he is even self-sacrificing: "the most active [settler] . . . neglecting his own lodgings to procure them for his comrades" (20).

And like the later frontiersman-guide figures in antebellum romance, at the end Smith in disgust leaves the settlement he has helped to create, which, ironically, has become a threat to the peace he has sought and found in the forest. Smith does not go farther west, unlike Natty Bumppo in *The Prairie* (1827) or Paulding's shepherd-hunter Ambrose Bushfield in *Westward Ho!* Instead, the captain returns east, to England

5. Paulding, *Letters from the South*, II,11; Marx, "Pastoralism in America," 43.

and London. Still, in Virginia he has always been happier in the forest and on the rivers than in the town. In Jamestown he is irritated by demands to mediate disputes, punish sloth, or fight rebellion. There he has to struggle against the ungrateful and dangerous malice of disaffected settlers who accuse him, of all people, of crimes against the colony. After dealing with such men, unfriendly Indians, or a maddened bear that drives three of his young followers from their rowboat, Smith the shepherd-rescuer can relax in the forest. The bear incident makes him laugh for the only time in Davis's account. Refreshed by the forest, Smith settles back in the retrieved boat, lights his pipe, and tells the story of his life as moss-hung trees glide by and the mockingbirds sing (116–18). Sweet idyll: such restful green interludes in *First Settlers* and later southern romances and tales represent the pastoral device of the restorative journey into the pleasant place. Outside, on the periphery, the real world forever waits, destructive and vile, pressing mutability upon Davis's dreamy, static Virginia idyll. This is his history lesson—the informative crux of his Jamestown pastoral.

Captain Argall, another historical English seaman and explorer, comes up the James River after Smith has left the unhappy settlement. European civilization encroaches upon the doomed "second Canaan," as Smith and many other explorers have called Virginia (59). Now the mockingbird's bright, soothing song, which Davis so delighted in describing, is replaced by a sad melody of loss sung by Pocahontas. The quiet, unexpected shadow of a hawk appears on the river. This is Davis's best image in the entire tale. Again, it is not especially unique, but it is apposite and surprising in context, as a good image should be.

After kidnapping Pocahontas to exchange her for the guns and equipment Powhatan has stolen from them, Argall's men pause on the river to feast on turkey they have shot on the banks. Here once more is Davis's softly lyric style—and something else as well: "It was an open spot. But before them was a forest of tall trees, and from tree to tree the long moss extended, waved by the noon-tide breeze. The steady breezes gently and continually rising and falling, filled the high lonesome forests with an awful reverential harmony, inexpressibly sublime, and not to be enjoyed anywhere but in those native Indian regions" (212). Subtly, Davis has replaced the song of the mockingbird with another, less cheerful sound: the melancholy soughing of wind in trees. The mood of the forest is no longer as pleasant or rejuvenating as it once could be. It has become "reverential," almost solemn. This new ambiance suggests that there is something holy about the forest. For Davis now its destruction seems to take on a quality of sacrilege. In that one phrase, "reverential harmony," his wilderness becomes sacred, adumbrating the enormity of Argall's mission. Argall is under orders to "burn all" if the Indians do not return the stolen property (219).

More poignancy is given to the tone of this fittingly but nonetheless unexpectedly melancholy forest interlude by the words of the song Pocahontas sings after everyone has eaten. It is an elegy to the doomed wilderness and the demise of its natives. She must have been Christianized very quickly and thoroughly to have learned Psalm 137 so well. In this scene, regardless of anything else he might have wished to show about the westernization of the Indian princess, Davis provides a dramatic device "peculiarly appropriate"—as he says himself—to a moment in history that pauses on the verge of the loss of innocence. Pocahontas sings: "'By the rivers of Babylon there we sat down. Yea, we wept when we remembered Zion. For they that carried us away captives, required of us a song; and they that wasted us, required of us mirth'" (213).

Nantaquas has undergone a depressing change. He appeared princely when Davis first introduced him; now he looks quite different. I do not think that Davis by any means intended for his appearance at the end of the romance to be taken as admirable or quaint. If Pocahontas is being civilized by the West, in a literary way at least, Nantaquas certainly is being brutalized by it. He has become a joke for the white men, almost but not entirely as pathetic as Cooper's debased Chingachgook called Indian John in *The Pioneers* (1832). Assimilation fits neither character. Wearing a soiled European shirt over his buckskins and Smith's cast-off lace hat cocked jauntily over one eye as the English sailors have taught him,

Nantaquas looks more like a posturing thug than an Indian prince (233, 252–53).

As Argall's ship proceeds on its cruise up-river, Davis describes a burned Indian village ashore. It belonged to a tribe that refused to join Powhatan in an effort to drive the English out of the land. Internecine fighting in Jamestown has found its counterpart in warfare among the Indians themselves. The narrative's increasing irony and pathos lie in how Davis continues to play upon the European classical pastoral conception of the New World as Argall's ship sails on. The barque glides between banks of huge sunlit trees. Indians follow along on the land while the white men look out into a veritable green paradise. On the surface this is a beautiful scene, as Indian maidens with baskets pick strawberries in the clearings.

Suddenly, however, there is a pause—the pastoral shudder. The moving sails and voices, as Argall very realistically gives orders aboard, become unexpectedly associated with the image of a fish hawk flying low over the water, seeking prey, and moving along with the ship. Davis skillfully has bracketed the action of *First Settlers* in an imagery of predatory birds that carries a double implication. Most obviously, the eagle and the hawk represent the commerce that has come with the English. Less obviously, the imagery reveals that Davis was not at all duped by his own pastoral nostalgia, or beguiled by the beautiful scenery he so lovingly describes. He was well aware of the cruel side of nature, of that "tiger heart" of Melville's that also beats beneath the "grassy glades" of Ishmael's pastoral rumination in *Moby-Dick* (1850). D. H. Lawrence saw this awareness of a conflict between good and evil in nature as a "rudimentary American vision."[6]

Davis handles his last and most impressive scene in *First Settlers* by mixing his hard style (the orders given by Argall) with his soft style (the bucolic dreamland ashore):

> They now weighed their anchor and stood up the river. The sun was approaching the meridian. A light breeze distending the canvas, enabled the tall ship to sail gently along the shore, covered with awful forests. . . . "Steady" was called by the captain, and re-

6. Herman Melville, *Moby-Dick; or, The Whale*, rpr. with introduction by Newton Arvin (New York, 1959), 484–85; D. H. Lawrence, *Studies in Classic American Literature* (New York, 1951), 35.

peated by the helmsman, while the echoes multiplied the sound on land. Every person had come on deck. The Indian princess was reclining against the quarter-rail, surrounded by Sir Thomas, West, Percy, Holcroft, etc. Captain Argall was pacing the deck, conning the ship by some point on land and either repeating "Steady so! Steady a-long!" or calling "Starboard a little! Mind your starboard helm!"

. . . Here and there the magnificent pine forests opening their vistas, discovered to the ravished eye meadows purpled with strawberries, flocks of turkies strolling about, and herds of deer wantonly prancing. Companies of young Indian girls were also seen, some busy gathering the rich fragrant fruit, and others, having already filled their baskets, reclining under the shade of the weeping willow. The nimble cat-fish sometimes jumped above the water, while the fish hawk hovered over the surface watching its prey. (218–19)

What is most surprising about this up-river journey is how closely it parallels F. Scott Fitzgerald's passionate concluding description in *The Great Gatsby* (1925) of Henry Hudson's trip up a northern river in 1609—almost the same time as Argall's in 1607. Davis fills in the nautical and geographical details Fitzgerald omits. The men of the *Half-Moon* also looked out in silent wonder, while Hudson no doubt gave commands to his helmsman, into a fresh green vision of Eden during another brief pause in time. For Davis as well as Fitzgerald the dream is overwhelmed by a ship, and furthermore scotched by a fish hawk, as the "active life" comes into the garden with the "busy hum of men" that he describes at the beginning of his tale (20–21). At the end *First Settlers* becomes a pastoral eulogy for the lost "race of Indians [that] has been destroyed by the inroads of the whites!" (273) Nantaquas has donned his dirty shirt and absurd hat. Indian villages have been burned, and not only by fellow Indians. Pocahontas is a prisoner of the English, and strawberry fields have been changed into tobacco plantations.

The moral lesson of Davis's romance, also evoked in Fitzgerald's image of the New World, is the vanity of human wishes. If he sounds particularly didactic in giving his message, it is because Davis was, after all, a teacher in America who had to make his history lessons clear. What happened to the Virginia Indians, he concludes, can happen to any civilization: "The cry of the hawk only is heard where the mock bird poured his melody; and no vestige is left behind of a powerful nation, who once . . . believed their strength invincible, and their race eternal!" (273) In its didacticism, images, and incidents, John Davis's *First Settlers of Virginia* sets the precedent for pastoral in the antebellum southern romance.

3

Some Other Versions of Southern Pastoral

In *Some Versions of Pastoral,* William Empson points out that the fundamental truths of the human condition with which pastoral deals are revealed in the "trick of style of its double plot." John Davis uses this trick to set the pace for antebellum pastoral in *The First Settlers of Virginia.* It imbues his and later idyllic imagery in southern literature with a quiet irony that is an inescapable part of the "counterpoising awareness of the limitations of pastoral values" in the arcadian vision of life, as Patrick Cullen explains early in his discussion of Renaissance pastoral. Withdrawal from the nonpastoral or urban world implies criticism of it. After Empson, Poggioli and now Ettin also agree that irony is a primary element in pastoral.[1] For Empson the idyll provides a social mirror that presents a notion of the inadequacy of life by juxtaposing the real with the ideal in its suggestive double plot. The "pastoral figure" in literature, Empson says—the sojourner or shepherd-frontiersman in antebellum southern romance, I will add—is ready "to be the critic." Never, however, will the skillful utilizer of pastoral allow this figure to state or represent anything so particularly as to leave himself and his creator open to objection.

In this way pastoral dualism can free readers' judgment as it has freed the writer's imagination to be after all the subtle commentator upon his times. Readers, Empson goes on to explain, need not identify with either of the levels of action or exposition in the story before them. They can simply allow

---

1. Empson, *Some Versions of Pastoral,* 210; Patrick Cullen, *Spenser, Marvell, and Renaissance Pastoral* (Cambridge, Mass., 1970), 3; Ettin, *Literature and the Pastoral,* 103–104, 115.

whatever impression they wish to set in from the literature. They can take what it poses as being inconsequential or serious.[2] By using pastoral devices in romances and tales, writers of the Old South were able to get away with a degree of social, economic, and even political criticism of their supersensitive region that otherwise might have earned them the public opprobrium of being sectionally disloyal and personally depraved.

In the *Recreations of George Taletell, F. Y. C.* (1822), for instance, Isaac E. Holmes of South Carolina is as much concerned with revealing the destructiveness of bad farming and neglect of property in the South as with creating a comfortingly idealized picture of the southern plantation. The critical irony of his double plot carries intimations of trouble in the South. The underlying social commentary here denies another southern idyll as Holmes juxtaposes a rural ideal with rural reality in South Carolina. Guy A. Cardwell has stated that *Recreations of George Taletell* is probably the first extensive treatment in southern fiction of the plantation house.[3] Seen in this light, it is also the first depiction by a southern author of the unlikeliness of the plantation retreat as an enduring, obtainable ideal.

In the pastoral manner of putting the complex into the simple, the surface action of *Recreations* is uncomplicated. George Taletell, a Charleston lawyer and politician—like Holmes himself—describes a December journey he takes along the Ashley River to his uncle's plantation for an old-fashioned Christmas holiday. On the road he makes some troubling observations. It is here, in the suggestiveness of George's reflections, that the story achieves its greatest depth of vision and value as social commentary. The reality through which Taletell passes is not as pleasant or as idyllic as the dream of southern rural retreat toward which he is traveling.

As he starts on his trip out of Charleston, Taletell thinks of the garden orderliness and beauty of the English countryside he once visited. Here Holmes is setting up his contrast—his

2. Empson, *Some Versions of Pastoral*, 19, 34, 53–54.
3. Guy A. Cardwell, "The Plantation House: An Analogical Image," *Southern Literary Journal*, II (Fall 1969), 5.

pastoral dilemma. In anticipation of the bucolic pleasures he knows he will experience at his uncle's rural retreat, George the traveler recalls another rural ideal in England—that of pleasingly located manor houses with sweeping views, and tidy villages with square church towers rising amid trees. He remembers having reflected at the time that all the man-made objects he saw seemed arranged to enhance the green and undulating beauty of the countryside. Becoming dreamy in his chaise, George slacks the reins and thinks of "the pleasures of a still and quiet life" on the land.[4]

In this story, though, Holmes is too much concerned with real issues to let his traveler indulge for long in mere pastoral reverie. Very cleverly and with evident irony, Holmes brings George back to reality: "So entirely rural were my feelings," he says, "that the cawing of the crow from the distant oak harmonized with them more entirely, than the mingled tones of many wind instruments" (31). A crow's cry is not at all harmonious or pastorally melodic. Holmes is making a point: the cry grates in the air. It is a startling, disharmonious crackle of the real world that brings Taletell back to the bumping of his chaise on the rough road and to some discomforting feelings. He is not, after all, passing through an English idyll, but rather through an actual, contemporary American countryside whose bucolic qualities are sadly tarnished. The landscape is unpleasing aesthetically and disrupted by heavy commerce on its roads:

> Yet a traveller is disappointed who, having heard of the richness of our lands, passes through the country along the public roads, which are laid out over extensive flats, or pine barrens—so that notwithstanding the beauty of the roads, a ride of many miles through the low country is felt to be monotonous. The neat cottage and trim garden, so cheering to the travellers along the English road, together with the roll of stage coaches and the rattling of post chaises, are entirely wanted to animate the ride, whilst a few log houses scattered over the sandy plain, together with the long lines of heavily laden wagons and jingling horse bells, but serve to make the scene more oppressively dreary. (32–33)

4. Isaac E. Holmes, *Recreations of George Taletell, F. Y. C.* (Charleston, 1822), 15–25. All references to the work will be taken from this edition and noted parenthetically by page number in the text.

Here is Holmes's critical perspective in his story, an un-complimentary commentary upon the real that he disguises at the end with his description of an idealized plantation, the *locus amoenus* toward which George is traveling. *Recreations* amounts to a criticism of too-rapid commercial growth and of the callous treatment of the land because of cotton specula-tion, an increasing internal slave trade, and bad farming practices. The pastoral sense of loss and mutability lies at the heart of Holmes's story. He makes certain of these points by creating first an English and then a plantation idyll to bracket George's journey through the truth. Neglected man-sion gardens are Holmes's major symbols for the passing of rural order and tranquility from southern American life as a commercial ethic replaces an agrarian one. Cotton rows have replaced the lawns, paths, shrubs, and trees of the di-lapidated old plantation houses George observes on his way. Adding to the dreariness is the December leaflessness of the trees that border the avenues leading to these once-great houses. In the barren branches the wind makes a music as solemn as John Davis's along the James. The sound accom-panies George's melancholy thoughts: "You may now visit on the banks of the Ashley, many splendid remains of former grandeur, extensive gardens, whose pendant willows bend in mournful silence over the still water of a neglected basin, and seem to weep its impoverished founts . . . [and] it is not un-common to see the snowy fleece of the cotton plant cheering the hopes of the young planter, on those very spots where his father walked among cooling shades and 'long protracted bowers'" (68–70).

For all the diverting holiday cheer of convivial celebration and merry hunts on the uncle's idyllic plantation, the careful reader cannot forget the slice of real, chaotic life with its im-ages of progress and change in ruined mansions and gardens through which George drives and through which he will have to pass again and again as he goes from dream to dream. Im-permanence, human restlessness, and the destructiveness of the commercial ethic are the issues Isaac Holmes really con-fronts in the *Recreations of George Taletell* while he evokes for the casual reader what was to become a familiar and comfort-ing picture in southern romance—the secure, tranquil, and happy plantation. What lies threateningly on its periphery, however, is what really counts in his tale of a Christmas diversion.

In "Seclusaval" (1839), on the other hand, the Reverend Dr. Henry Ruffner, a Virginia clergyman and educator, weaves a pastoral pattern that seems to be a *reductio ad absurdum* of the form. It also appears to justify Lewis P. Simpson's comment about the essentially reactionary and escapist qualities of pastoral in the literature of the Old South. The nineteenth-century southern literary mind, he writes in *The Dispossessed Garden*, "sought to symbolize its opposition to modernity in an image of pastoral permanence."[5] This is so only up to a point. Even in a story as slight as *Recreations of George Taletell*, traditional pastoral imagery in southern fiction of the nondomestic sort is always undercut, confronted by a counterbalancing imagery of actual life that gives idyll the lie. Writers of antebellum southern romances of the kind I am discussing face real issues through their pastoral devices. Even Ruffner in "Seclusaval" confronts an issue, although he is not as physiocratic about it as the other writers are. His concern is more psychological than material, as he deals in his story with the problem of religious bigotry and the pain and guilt it causes.

Under the surface of the withdrawn, perfect idyll it depicts, "Seclusaval" is disturbingly neurotic and pictorially oppressive. Bucolic imagery in the story recalls the order and odor of funeral flowers, the yew-shaped landscaping of monumental nineteenth-century cemeteries, and the evocation of the grave in Böcklin's painting, *The Isle of the Dead*. It could very well be that the stifling pastoral perspectives in "Seclusaval" influenced Edgar Allan Poe's nightmare of bucolic confinement in "The Domain of Arnheim" (1847). There the heavily perfumed air, "dream-like" trees, and incredible "semi-Gothic, semi-Saracenic" architecture seem to be the handiwork of sylphs, fairies, genii, or gnomes. Like the protagonist Garame of Ruffner's story, Ellison, the landscape architect behind Poe's pastoral aberration, wants to mold an impossibly per-

---

5. Lewis P. Simpson, *The Dispossessed Garden: Pastoral and History in Southern Literature* (Athens, Ga., 1975), 70.

fect garden free of nature's disproportions. One of Poe's biographers, Arthur Hobson Quinn, explains that Poe was ill and depressed when he wrote "The Domain of Arnheim." According to Richard Wilbur, it is a story, like so many others he wrote, that indicates Poe's recurrent wish to withdraw from personal troubles and earthly cares into a safely—however weirdly—circumscribed dream-realm.[6] What Garame turns from in "Seclusaval," with an eerie immediacy, is a workaday world in which he has made a fortune among some of the coarsest and most ill-disposed people on earth, and a recollection of his human failure in having denied his true love because she is a Jew.

"Seclusaval" is a sequel to Ruffner's other story, "Judith Bensaddi." Curtis C. Davis points out that this is probably the first American fiction to deal with the minority issue posed by Jews in the United States.[7] In the story, Garame, a William and Mary law student at the time, meets Judith and her brother Eli on a cruise. After Eli accidentally drowns at sea, Garame consoles Judith and they fall in love. When she goes back to England with his proposal of marriage, he returns to his Shenandoah Valley home where he begins to worry about how his community will react to Judith's being a Jew. He imagines his peers will not approve of her. Actually, the problem lies in his own doubts about her heritage rather than in the untried community. Conveniently, he blames his own hesitancy to wed Judith on society and drops her. She is heartbroken, of course, and eventually marries another.

"Seclusaval" continues the story of Garame, who has never been content since his bad treatment of Judith. Now a successful attorney, he has made a fortune litigating and digging in the Georgia gold fields. This grim area of uneasy settlement, rapacity, and murder was described realistically by William Gilmore Simms in *Guy Rivers*, published five years before "Seclusaval." It is from this ugly world that Garame at

6. Edgar Allan Poe, *The Complete Works*, ed. James A. Harrison (16 vols.; New York, 1902), V,184; Arthur Hobson Quinn, *Edgar Allan Poe: A Critical Biography* (New York, 1942), 528–31; Richard Wilbur, "The House of Poe," in *Anniversary Lectures* (Library of Congress, Washington, D.C., 1959), 24–25.

7. Curtis C. Davis, "'Judith Bensaddi' and the Reverend Doctor Henry Ruffner," *Publications of the American Jewish Historical Society*, XXXIX (September 1949–June 1950), 117.

first seems to be retreating. In reality, he is only trying to get away from himself, to make atonement for his bigotry in monastic retreat in the sealed-off Vale of Seclusa in the Virginia mountains not far from the gold fields. After purchasing the vale, which he discovers by accident, he hires a gardener to create a park there. Coincidentally, Judith, now a widow, comes to the vicinity of Seclusaval as a music teacher in the school Garame has endowed. They meet, marry, and retire to the transformed valley.

In its original wild state, Seclusaval looks to Garame like a "terrestrial paradise," a familiar term for Virginia's untouched landscape. Typically, too, he thinks that it requires "only the hand of man to prune and dress its profusion, to make it outvie all the pastoral beauties of Arcadia in the golden age." What conscience-ridden Garame sees in Seclusaval is another and earlier version of Poe's demented Arnheim: "a hiding place from the storms of life," Garame thinks, from which he can "look forth upon the outer world of insatiate passions and self-tormenting hearts."[8] This is self-revelation rather than smugness in Garame, and it lends the story its psychological dimension. He had adjusted very well to that outer world he seems now to scorn. His urge to get away from it all reflects self-loathing that he wants to bury somehow in a dream of Arcady.

Under the direction of Baylor, Garame's imported English gardener, Seclusaval is tidied and transformed. It assumes the "appearance of a park. Whatever was unpleasant to the eye was disappearing from the noble woods; sweet lawns, winding and branching in various ways . . . opened to the eye . . . the most delightful views of trees, hills, and mountains on every side" (643). This erasure of nature's disproportions is the symbolical purging of Garame's conscience, an impossible cleansing of the order of things. To his woods and lawns he adds "a shepherd's cot . . . a romantic place at the foot of a precipice, on the opposite side of the valley, for I designed to give little of my beautiful grounds to the plow; but to make

<hr/>

8. Henry Ruffner, "Seclusaval; or, The Sequel to the Tale of 'Judith Bensaddi,'" *Southern Literary Messenger*, V (October 1839), 641. All references to the work will be taken from this edition and noted parenthetically by page number in the text.

Seclusaval a pastoral scene, where flocks and herds might graze . . . and the sounds of the shepherd's pipe might mingle with the song of birds and the chime of waterfalls" (643).

This work is all cosmetic, an overlay on nature: "enchantment," as Judith herself says when she sees the garden, a mere "sweet image of paradise" (659, 662). Like Prospero in *The Tempest*, Garame cannot keep the real world and human responsibility at bay in a magical re-creation of Eden. The perspectives in Seclusaval all seem to end in mystery, in hidden places where something dreadful could lurk—something in nature, something in the mind: "Lawns here and there permitted the eye to penetrate into the bosom of the park, and afforded glimpses of beautiful groves and retreats, that enticed the imagination as much by what was hidden as by what was revealed" (651).

It is here, in these hidden areas of the garden that so entice the mind, that Ruffner's pastoral, like all the others, works against itself. Something else comes in from these darker reaches to disturb Seclusaval's repose, whether Ruffner intends this or not. It occurs in the echo of the "Echoing Glen" hidden at the grotto end of Garame's artificial lake. With the orderly, trimmed garden to enfold him, Garame might well feel free of further responsibilities and remorse. Jubilantly he shows off the glen, blowing a bugle that elicits a horrible sound from the darkness—a harsh, discordant echo, a mockery in cacophony of the neatly contrived pastoral forms Garame and Baylor have created. The echo sounds "as if ten-thousand shrill-mouthed demons have set up a yell" (662). In this surprising intrusion from the grotto a vestige of Caliban appears in Ruffner's idyll. In the ugly echo Ruffner, however unwittingly, makes his concession to that basically Manichean concept of a good-bad dichotomy Americans see in nature, as Lawrence has it in *Studies in Classic American Literature*. The echo's discord, furthermore, recalls the disharmonies of the hard life in those Georgia gold fields at the periphery of Seclusaval. This recollection of reality at the end mocks the artificial harmonies that fallible Garame-Ruffner has created as a vain symbol of pastoral permanence in a changing, dangerous world.

A more standard contrapuntal pattern of antebellum pastoral emerges in the writing of James Kirke Paulding. Like his acquaintance William Gilmore Simms, Paulding was essentially a realist in a romantic, sentimental age. He took a sharp look at life and events going on around him, and commented upon them with concern and disappointment. His biographer Amos L. Herold mentions that although Paulding was a New Yorker, his heart was in the South, particularly in Virginia. With his beloved "great West," as he wrote in a letter, "the depository in which is to be cherished and preserved the genuine characteristics of Americans," Paulding felt the South stood as a bastion against the growing industrialization of nineteenth-century America. He used pastoral to comment pointedly about this; there is nothing escapist in his juxtapositions. Vernon Louis Parrington labels Paulding a Jeffersonian in the fundamentals of his social creed—in his physiocratic leanings, his deep distrust of all middle-class programs, and his preference for simple country ways over city economies. Paulding felt that one feature of American life in need of rectification—as Alexander Cowie writes in his account of the rise of the American novel—was the "trend toward urban life with all its attendant evils of speculation and capitalistic exploitation of the working classes."[9] This conviction lies at the heart of alternating scenes of idyll and loss of idyll that occur in his literary descriptions of the South and Southwest.

The South repaid Paulding for his affinity. His publications remained popular there while they were being forgotten in the North. In 1855 he wrote a letter in which he said that although "in the North I cannot boast of any great popularity, I have many warm friends in the South, and have been more than once applied to by Southerners in the quarter to know where my works could be purchased." He was, for instance, admired by Simms as a "downright sensible writer, hearty, frank, and unaffected."[10] In 1854 Simms wrote to Paulding as-

9. Amos L. Herold, *James Kirke Paulding: Versatile American* (1926; rpr. New York, 1966), 2, 109; James Kirke Paulding, *The Letters of James Kirke Paulding*, ed. Ralph M. Aderman (Madison, 1962), 189–90; Vernon Louis Parrington, *The Romantic Revolution in America, 1800–1860* (New York, 1927), 214; Alexander Cowie, *The Rise of the American Novel* (New York, 1948), 195.
10. Paulding, *Letters*, 533; William Gilmore Simms, *The Letters of William Gilmore Simms*, ed. Mary C. Simms Oliphant, Alfred Taylor Odell, T. C.

suring him of the South's regard: "You are too well known, and too much honored in the South . . . than to be thought of as a foe of the South" (Simms, *Letters*, III, 335–36). Such affinity and acceptance are sufficient justification for placing James Kirke Paulding among the romancers of the antebellum South.

Each of the two Paulding works I will discuss involves a search for an American Eden in the South or Southwest, and the dream of realizing there the Jeffersonian concept of a functional rural American middle ground of productive farms, lying between the extremes of urban corruption and wilderness barbarity. Technology and commercial exploitation of the land turn out to be the counterbalances to this dream, and Paulding does not enjoy the solace even of the idealized plantations that occur in *Recreations of George Taletell* and later in John Pendleton Kennedy's *Swallow Barn*. In his critical honesty, and to his personal dismay, Paulding is forced to admit that the machine and the innovators will triumph. For such a realist there can be no withdrawal from this harsh fact and no denial of the world outside, no matter what Lewis P. Simpson has to say in retrospect about the escapist use of idyllic imagery in the romances of the Old South. In his American "epic" poem *The Backwoodsman* (1818), which tells the story of farmer Basil's move from the Hudson Valley to the West, Paulding writes bitterly that it is man himself in the final analysis who is the "serpent of this blooming Paradise."[11] He sounds almost as misanthropic as Ruffner's Garame, and as pessimistic as Simms.

The fictionalized *Letters from the South* (1817) is the result of Paulding's trip in the summer of 1816 from Norfolk to the Virginia mineral springs inland. The book is a series of random essays loosely held together by the device of having been written by a first-time Yankee traveler in the South to a friend in a northern city. Paulding's traveler is a good example of

---

Duncan Eaves, introduction by Donald Davidson (5 vols.; Columbia, S.C., 1952–56), II,30n. All references to Simms's letters will be taken from this edition and noted parenthetically by volume and page number in the text.

11. James Kirke Paulding, *The Backwoodsman: A Poem* (Philadelphia, 1818), 36–37.

Empson's pastoral figure who provides a mechanism for critical perspective in a piece of literature. He is also typical of an innovation in the nineteenth-century pastoral traveler that Robin Magowan has described in an essay. This traveler is not an exile stumbling into a rejuvenating arcadian retreat; rather, he is a vacationer of leisure and good humor who identifies sympathetically with a bucolic environment he has entered. Idyllic evocations in his report contain their criticism by the contrast they pose to the outside world from which he has come. Looking over well-tilled southern fields along his way in, Paulding's traveler states his author's theme of the superiority of the rural to the urban life: "No wonder that the cultivators of the land are those who constitute the real wholesome strength and virtue of every civilized country; since they daily look to the Heavens and to the earth alone for their support."[12]

The traveler reflects that trade and industry, along with bad farming, have done their share to harm the Tidewater plantations (I, 41–42). The landscape beyond the Piedmont grows invitingly pastoral. Details in Paulding's description of the valley of Virginia adhere to the formula for the southern *locus amoenus* in other antebellum writings, featuring neat farms, rolling meadows, grazing herds, and animated waters all enclosed by softly enfolding trees and mountains. The morning mist that had lain like a great body of water over the scene rolls away, and the traveler is delighted by what he sees:

> The imaginary sea became a fertile valley, extending up and down, as far as the eye could reach. In the midst of the green foliage of oaks and solemn pines, were seen rich and cultivated lands, and comfortable farm-houses, surrounded by ruddy fields of clover, speckled with groups of cattle grazing in its luxuriant pastures, or reposing quietly among its blossoms. . . . Here was seen a little town, and near it a field, animated with sturdy labourers. In one place two little rivers, after winding and coquetting through the meadows, sometimes approaching, sometimes receding, some-

12. Robin Magowan, "Fromentin and Jewett: Pastoral Narrative in the Nineteenth Century," *Comparative Literature*, XVI (1964), 334–35; Paulding, *Letters from the South*, I,140. All references to the work will be taken from this edition and noted parenthetically by volume and page number in the text.

times hid, and sometimes seen, joined their currents, and finally disappeared in the distant woods, beyond which a high peaked cliff, towering above the ascending vapours, glittered in the beams of the morning sun, like a giant capped with a helmet of burnished gold. It seemed as if a new and blooming world was gradually emerging from chaos, and assuming the most beautiful arrangement, under the hand of some invisible agent in the mist of morning. (I, 90)

Sitting in a country church near Staunton on a Sunday morning, the traveler looks outside on a stream and mountain view that provide a "path for man's thoughts to ascend to heaven!" Going outside, he thinks, "I don't know how it is, but there is something in the repose of the country, and particularly in the silence and shade of deep groves, that is allied to religious emotions by some inscrutable tie. Perhaps it is because almost every subject we see in the country is the work of Deity, and every object common to cities the work of man" (II, 67–68).

But there is a Marvellian winged chariot hurrying up behind Paulding's vacationer as he goes farther inland. This is symbolized by the settler's axe he hears that "is like a whirlwind, which levels the tallest trees of the forest in a twinkling." Americans are like Indians, the traveler comments, who pull up stakes and move on to new hunting grounds when the old are depleted (I, 71–72). As usual in antebellum pastoral, disillusionment and bitterness entwine themselves into Paulding's transitory idylls. At one point his traveler complains in fatalistic disgust that "every thing in this country has been, for two centuries at least, growing downwards, like unto a cow's tail" (II, 61).

Worse than the American waste of the land in unconscionable development, to Paulding's far-seeing eye, was the unsightly technological progress that was also spawned of cities. For many Americans the steam engine was regarded as a positive symbol of progress in the first half of the nineteenth century, as Kenneth J. La Budde points out. For Paulding, as for Hawthorne at Sleepy Hollow, Thoreau at Walden, and Cooke at Martinsburg, it was a terrifying and disruptive new force that ruined the tranquility and configuration of the landscape and deprived humanity of freedom and dignity. Further stimulated into criticism of the outside world by the pastoral environment around him, the traveler writes that the "vulgar profusion" of goods produced by factories lured people away from the virtue-imparting soil into the evil cities, "to the exclusion of every nobler pursuit and all rational economy" (I, 49). As Gerald E. Gerber suggests, Paulding may be the first significant American writer to use the image of a machine as a composite sign of degenerate times.[13] He does so particularly in a surprising image in *Letters from the South.* One night in the peaceful bucolic setting of Fincastle, Virginia, the traveler unexpectedly has a nightmare of a barren "Isle of Machines" whose superior beings are steam-powered engines. Whereas in Fincastle the people have found rural contentment and prosperity by carefully taming the wilderness and creating attractive farms that harmonize with the natural surroundings, in the dream human beings have been debased and made obsolete by labor-saving machines they themselves have created (II, 20–27).

The ideas that occur in *Letters from the South* appear with greater force in Paulding's romance, *Westward Ho!* (1832). According to Ernest E. Leisy, this is one of the best nineteenth-century depictions of frontier life in Kentucky. Simms was so pleased with the book that he wrote to Paulding in 1839, calling him "one of the fathers of our forest literature,—a leading Pioneer" (Simms, *Letters,* I, 144). The theme of *Westward Ho!* at first seems to be the possibility of human redemption in the Southwest—pastoral rejuvenation of spirit and reorientation of values to be obtained there on "the extremest verge of the civilized world. Beyond was all forests, and wild Indians. . . . It was a region of danger, of adventure, of romance . . . this wild and dangerous solitude."[14] The action involves the jour-

13. Kenneth J. La Budde, "The Rural Earth: Sylvan Paradise," *American Quarterly,* X (Summer 1958), 153; Henry David Thoreau, *Walden and Other Writings,* ed. Brooks Atkinson (New York, 1950), 105–107; Gerald E. Gerber, "James Kirke Paulding and the Image of the Machine," *American Quarterly,* XXII (Fall 1970), 741.

14. Ernest E. Leisy, *The American Historical Novel* (Norman, Okla., 1950), 115; James Kirke Paulding, *Westward Ho! A Tale* (2 vols.; New York, 1832), I,66. All references to the work will be taken from this edition and noted parenthetically by volume and page number in the text.

ney of Cuthbert Dangerfield away from a decadent Virginia plantation civilization to the untried Kentucky frontier. He is a good-natured but profligate Tidewater planter who loses his estate on a bet. In making his point, Paulding depicts Dangerfield as being a little relieved by his bad luck. Going into the new country with him and his cavalcade of wagons and slaves are his forgiving wife, his lovely daughter Virginia, and his comically indolent cousin Littlejohn, a prototype of the incurably wasteful southern aristocrat.

Traveling on the flooding Ohio River to his new plantation, Dangerfield and his family pass through an untouched country that "teemed with danger and death . . . [and] melancholy, yet was delightful" (I, 74), words that lend more credence to Lawrence's observation upon the American Manichean view of nature. Then the travelers arrive at a "spot where the strata of rocks disappeared, and a paradise of nature opened to their view . . . an open forest of gigantic trees." Here grew no underbrush on the "shady meadows and the whole was one carpet of blossoms opening to the spring air" (I, 84). They settle in this natural Eden, and the garden's inadvertent ruination begins while Dangerfield's character is restored. The family erect their tents on the grass, and the flowers there are covered by a functional dun canvas.

When trees are cut "the first wound [is] given to the primeval forest" (I, 87). Paulding writes here in a voice that has its precedent in another frontier romance of five years earlier, in the bitter response Cooper assigns to Natty Bumppo as the old hunter watches Ishmael Bush cut down a tree for fuel in *The Prairie*. It is a dilemma that Simms also faced in fiction in his turn: in order to create a town or a farm, trees have to be cleared, cut, or girdled, and the landscape must be made ugly for a while. To this inevitability in the American realization of new beginnings, Simms and other writers always provide a wistful pastoral counterbalance. For Paulding in *Westward Ho!* it occurs in the original site of Dangerfieldville, which was to undergo drastic change where at first there "was such a little paradise as whilom the shepherds haunted in the pastorals once so admired, but now eschewed as fantastic pictures of a state of society which never had an existence. So much the worse, so much the worse; for to us it seems that the very beau ideal of human happiness would consist in this imaginary union . . . of all the simplicity of rural innocence, all the mild excitements of rural scenes, rural amusements, and rural occupations, with gentle manners and intellectual refinement" (II, 11).

Enough of dreaming. Paulding has not succumbed to the idle, escapist pastoral mood Henry Ruffner displayed in "Seclusaval." From his bedroom window at the Dangerfield house after settlement, a young visitor named Dudley Rainsford looks out upon a startling and depressing scene of destruction—the very realistically depicted process of clearing the forest for cultivation. "The lofty girdled trees, stripped of their foliage, and bristling the surrounding fields like the tall masts of first-rate men-of-war, gave an air of desolation to the landscape, which was bounded at a distance by a dark wall of gloomy forest" (I, 108).

Another of the ironic dichotomies in Paulding's Kentucky bucolic spot is the way in which Dangerfield's good character is restored with a frontiersman's help while the idyll is being ruined. He has to be active and resourceful once again in order to survive. His character "resumed that native sagacity and vigour which wealth, indulgence, and, above all, idleness had lulled to sleep. . . . His mind rose with the exigencies of the occasion" (II, 39). Dangerfield is aided in his labors of clearing, building, planting, and hunting by Ambrose Bushfield, a native of North Carolina. Bushfield is Paulding's contribution to the type of the capable, sturdy, reliable frontiersman or shepherd-guide in antebellum southern romance that started with Davis's John Smith. Like Smith of *First Settlers*, Bushfield is "free as the air he breathed . . . hardy as the trees of the primeval forests . . . not ignorant or vulgar" (I, 68).

When the Dangerfields leave their forest-bound plantation in Kentucky on a river trip to New Orleans, they are surprised to see on the banks all the plats, villages, and roads that have been cut hastily and carelessly into the woods. Such evidence of human progress in the New World is reminiscent of the ugliness of Dangerfield's own girdled trees. Other settlers following after him are doing what he had to do, and there is not much of the revitalizing forest left anymore (I, 130). In

Louisiana their gentlemanly old French host complains of the Yankee tendency to speculative development and business enterprise that has wrecked the idyllic calm and rural prosperity of his own village. He is Paulding's spokesman to be sure when he laments that nowadays "one has nothing to do . . . but to work all day to be only as comfortable as we used to be without working at all" (I, 135).

Bushfield's plight at the end of *Westward Ho!* is sardonically comic when he complains about it. Paulding is very serious, however, in his representation of the aspect of the free American spirit the frontiersman denotes, and in what the reader is to infer from the frontiersman's futility. Because he discovers a neighbor only five miles away from his cabin, Bushfield complains of feeling physically restricted in the vicinity of Dangerfieldville. He wants to "live independent" (II, 181, 183). Gray and tired like Natty Bumppo in *The Prairie*, Bushfield moves farther west in search of his elusive dream of freedom from land development and commercial activity, "somewhere in the vicinity of one of our most remote military posts on the Missouri" (II, 193). Disruptive civilization will catch up with him here just as it caught Cuthbert Dangerfield in his Kentucky retreat.

In Bushfield's death, alone and confused "in the interminable vastness of space" on the plains (II, 194), there is a hint of the American naturalism to come in Stephen Crane's *fin-de-siècle* depictions of the bemused little man lost in and defeated by the incomprehensible forces of an indifferent universe. But, in the Empsonian sense, readers can make up their own minds about it all. Paulding's pastoral devices evoke an American idyll. Then he creates other images and events that depict its defilement by human activity. Readers can decide for themselves whether Paulding is being picturesque in his story, in the way of so much popular romance of the day, or whether he is making a serious commentary upon the failure of Jeffersonian ideals in America.

4

John Pendleton Kennedy
and the Locus Amoenus

Pastoral interludes and contrasting nonpastoral scenes in *The First Settlers of Virginia* and *Westward Ho!* create descriptive counterbalances of stasis or rural calm, and change or human activity. Seemingly timeless secular southern Edens are opposed by the business of restless people who move in, bringing mutability and death with them. Time, C. Hugh Holman observes in *The Roots of Southern Writing*, is a "frightful entity" for many southern authors. The inescapability of time in modern pastoral is embodied in the epitaph "Et in Arcadia Ego" ("Even in Arcadia am I") inscribed on a sepulcher in Arcady and topped by a skull in a seventeenth-century painting by Guercino. With the imprimatur of Renato Poggioli, Erwin Panofsky has argued with final authority that these words are spoken by Death.[1] They attest an antipastoral or antipagan comprehension of the essential temporality of idyllic imagery in art. Thus pastoral in the West, Poggioli says, has become a Christian pastoral of death—again, the loss of Eden. Pastoral nostalgia in literature of the antebellum South can evoke an aesthetic shudder as well as reveal an authorial dilemma in longing for an idyllic rural existence in the face of contemporary realities. Shudder and dilemma are both evident in the uncongeniality of cold horticultural form and misanthropic psychological motive in Garame's hermitage in the Vale of Seclusa, especially when the unavoidable other, dynamic side

1. Hugh Holman, *The Roots of Southern Writing* (Athens, Ga., 1972), 14, 87; Poggioli, *The Oaten Flute*, 20–21; Erwin Panofsky, "'Et in Arcadia Ego': Poussin and the Elegiac Tradition," in Eleanor Terry Lincoln (ed.), *Pastoral and Romance: Modern Essays in Criticism* (Englewood Cliffs, N.J., 1969), 25–46.

of life intrudes into the funerary garden with determined hostility in that surprising echo that sounds like thousands of freed demons bent on destruction. Pastoral dilemma and pastoral shudder crop up too in the romances of John Pendleton Kennedy.

Kennedy was a cultivated attorney and politician from Baltimore. Quiet, orderly Virginia country life had as great an appeal for him as it did for James Kirke Paulding. Two of Kennedy's biographers, Charles H. Bohner and J. V. Ridgely, point out, however, that he also admired his city's business community, commerce, and progressiveness in supporting national internal improvements.[2] So Kennedy's pastoral imagery in his best romances develops into a joke in *Swallow Barn* (1832), but is deeply troubled in *Horse-Shoe Robinson* (1835). In an era of growing national drift—largely represented by the rise of socially leveling Jacksonian democracy, unseemly urban and rural development and mechanization, and abrasive North-South sectionalism—Kennedy in reaction became drawn to the peaceful Jeffersonian concept of the self-sustaining agricultural middle ground. The roots and realization of this ideal occur for him in a pre–Industrial Revolution economy represented not by Virginia's Swallow Barn plantation, but rather by Allen Musgrove's North Carolina farm in *Horse-Shoe Robinson*. Before his physiocratic leanings got the upper hand, Kennedy revealed an unpastoral conviction that although rural life could be stable and secure on the surface, it also could be conducive to isolation and ignorance. This is so in his depiction of Swallow Barn. Like Simms, Kennedy was an active man who had to admit, for better or worse, approve of it or not, that change was true to American social and economic patterns of his time.

Swallow Barn seems to be a gentle pastoral idealization of the southern plantation, written in the amiable, easy style and episodic structure of Washington Irving's *Sketch Book* (1820). Paulding was greatly impressed by the descriptions of rural Virginia in Kennedy's romance. Obviously unaware of

2. Charles H. Bohner, *John Pendleton Kennedy: Gentleman from Baltimore* (Baltimore, 1961), 116–18; J. V. Ridgely, *John Pendleton Kennedy* (New York, 1966), 30–31, 60–61.

the book's subtly vicious criticism of the plantation way of life in the South, Paulding wrote to his own publisher, Henry C. Carey, saying, with unconscious relevance to Kennedy's ironic scheme, that *Swallow Barn* gave a picture of country life in the South "drawn from Nature." In a letter to Kennedy himself, an equally beguiled Simms expressed the same approval (Simms, *Letters*, III, 122–23). Almost two decades after the Civil War, John Esten Cooke was similarly taken in. He wrote in his history of Virginia that *Swallow Barn* was the "best picture of Virginia country life in literature."[3]

On the dark other side of Kennedy's ostensible plantation idyll at Swallow Barn lie some uncomfortable historical facts that make the romance much more than the "comic pastoral" Charles H. Bohner calls it, or the mere "Southern Arcadia" of Lewis P. Simpson. In the development of antebellum southern pastoral, *Swallow Barn* as a work of literature is more significant than its own author makes it seem in the humorously self-deprecating and intentionally misleading preface to the first edition. Here he writes that "my book has but little philosophy to recommend it, and much less depth of observation."[4] Kennedy had far more insight and narrative skill than his statement admits. He wanted his romance of American life to be read, enjoyed, and approved in the South as well as the North. He wanted to make an impact without putting himself on the spot as another harping Yankee critic of southern ways. William Empson would approve of the pastoral mechanisms Kennedy uses to let his readers make up their own minds about what he is saying in his work. Kennedy is far less secretive about his intentions in *Horse-Shoe Robinson*, written a couple of years later.

The unobtrusive philosophical point Kennedy makes with humorous acceptance in *Swallow Barn*, and later with reactionary bitterness in *Horse-Shoe Robinson*, is that time, change, and death are the normal course of human events and

---

3. Paulding, *Letters*, 122; John Esten Cooke, *Virginia: A History of the People* (Boston, 1884), 496.

4. Bohner, *John Pendleton Kennedy*, 83; Simpson, *The Dispossessed Garden*, 44; John Pendleton Kennedy, *Swallow Barn; or, a Sojourn in the Old Dominion* (2 vols.; Philadelphia, 1832), I,viii.

cannot be made to stand still in a southern garden or anywhere else. His rather crotchety switch of attitude in *Horse-
Shoe Robinson* was largely due to his disappointment in the
direction in which Jacksonian democracy had taken the country.[5] Reflecting this, in the new preface to the 1851 edition of
Swallow Barn, Kennedy comments with regret on the kind of
social and economic "progress" that is breaking in on the
uniquely character-building insularity and "distinctive habits and modes of life" of the countryside. He further wonders
if the resulting "insipidity of character" is worth the loss of
the old "rough but pleasant flavor" of American types.[6] But
the text of *Swallow Barn* remains perforce to speak for itself.
In terms of my study there is no significant difference, except
for a heightening of Mark's eagerness to get away from the
plantation at the end, between the first edition of 1832 and
the casually and unsystematically, even reluctantly, revised
version Kennedy prepared twenty years later (x–xi). For the
sake of narrative continuity, a penultimate chapter giving an
idealized overview of the life of Captain John Smith was
dropped entirely. According to another biographer, Edward
M. Gwathmey, who quotes Kennedy's friend and fellow lawyer John H. B. Latrobe on the matter, Kennedy felt this hero-
worshiping sketch was only "'makeshift,'" an error of literary
padding.[7]

If in his 1851 preface Kennedy expresses *ex post facto* regret
at the incursions of progress into the southern garden, his
unchanged spokesman Mark Littleton in the romance feels
the reverse. He is Kennedy's sojourner in the pastoral place.
Littleton speaks for a less disillusioned Kennedy when he perceives that the people of the plantation need some restorative
breaths of outside air if they and their rural environment are
to survive in the modern world. His criticism is more or less

5. Bohner, *John Pendleton Kennedy*, 71, 119–23; Ridgely, *John Pendleton
Kennedy*, 74–75, 115.
6. John Pendleton Kennedy, *Swallow Barn; or, A Sojourn in the Old Dominion* (1853; rpr. with introduction by William S. Osborne, New York, 1962),
8–9. All references to the work will be taken from this edition and noted parenthetically by page number in the text.
7. Edward M. Gwathmey, *John Pendleton Kennedy* (New York, 1931),
102–103.

disguised, of course, because he appears to be another character in the type of the good-natured, appreciative nineteenth-
century traveler who comes into the *locus amoenus* to comment on life outside. Through Mark's wry observations of
Swallow Barn plantation ways, however, the pastoral criticism in this romance is directed toward the idyll and not toward the counterbalancing active world on its periphery.

When Mark Littleton comes on vacation to Swallow Barn
at the invitation of Ned Hazard, his cousin, the plantation is
being operated for the time being by Ned's brother-in-law
Frank Meriwether. The bad management by Ned's deceased
father and his predecessors had almost ruined the place. Characters whom Mark meets at his refuge and describes with such
ostensibly sympathetic good humor are comic types: Chub,
the pedantic parson-teacher; Philpot Wart, the crusty fox-
hunting lawyer; Meriwether himself, the patient gentleman-
farmer; dreamy, irresponsible Ned Hazard, who is heir to the
plantation; and his equally impractical, beautiful fiancée Bel
Tracy, daughter of litigious Isaac Tracy, owner of a neighbor-
ing plantation, The Brakes. In the way of nineteenth-century
romance, the names of these characters reveal their person-
alities and functions in the story. Frank's surname, for instance, suggests a phase of good times in fair weather. The
surname of Ned the inheritor suggests danger, chance, a hazard of good fortune.

In describing his host, Mark mentions a certain "reckless
expression" in Ned's character that is heightened by his jaunty
German forage cap and "the half swagger with which he
strikes his boot with his riding whip" (51). His careless manner recalls what Ambrose Dangerfield must have been like as
a wastrel youth before his frontier conversion to serious behavior in *Westward Ho!*, or the devil-may-care attitude of his
unreformed cousin Littlejohn. Ned is less interested in help-
ing Meriwether manage Swallow Barn than in organizing
household theatricals where the slaves are taught to provide
the special sound effects (98–99). His playful exuberance is
further expressed with a touch of scorn for art when he mocks
the voices and attitudes of opera singers of both sexes while
walking in the woods with Littleton (81–84). This is all winning, but awfully immature.

Worst of all is his thoughtlessness for those under him. This is shown when he frees an opossum his slaves have treed during a night hunt, and so deprives them of a welcome feast and diversion of their own (410–11). But the slaves at Swallow Barn are only pleasant, contented, and servile retainers and workers. There is one exception, Abe, and Kennedy interjects his story. No supporter of slavery, Kennedy shows how commendably a black man can behave away from the slave quarters. Son of a slave named Lucy and something of a sullen troublemaker at home, handsome Abe is sent out of the pastoral place off to sea where he sails well and dies bravely in a stormy Chesapeake rescue attempt. Lucy goes mad with grief waiting for his return. Otherwise, life goes on as before at Swallow Barn.

When Ned—this boyish, inconsiderate future master of the plantation—courts Bel Tracy, Littleton finally disparages him by commenting on how he acts the part of the "harebrained cavalier" (414). He is more of a "jesting careless" companion to her than a lover. Another of Ned's friends remarks to Littleton that, unless Ned becomes more serious in his attentions to Bel, he will lose her (237). For her part Bel displays "certain romantic fancies," Littleton observes, that do little to help Hazard keep his feet on the ground (228). With notions of medieval sport on her mind—derived needless to say from the usual source, Sir Walter Scott—Bel tries to tame a hawk for falconry. She and Ned fail in this episode, another in the series of events that reveal a disarming but foreboding incompetence in the two. Neither is likely to carry on the stabilizing good work of practical Meriwether on their joined plantations after they marry and Meriwether has died. For the acute reader, the inevitability of Ned's inheritance tempers the image of bucolic security in the Swallow Barn idyll.

At the heart of Kennedy's double plot in *Swallow Barn* is an advocacy of the worthwhile material and cultural advances of his day that could bring about social and intellectual enlightenment or a healthy broadening of attitude in a community's leaders. In view of this, he is less genial than mocking in the way he has Littleton depict the stubborn small-mindedness and parochialism of his two southern lords of the manor, Meriwether and Tracy. The physical and spiritual limitations imposed by isolated plantation life in the South, Kennedy points out here, can severely circumscribe perspective and activity even in people of leisure and means. Meriwether's ill-informed opinion about the progress being made in America's transportation system, for example, reduces him to an expression of futile reactionary petulance. He criticizes the U.S. railways for the greater national consolidation they portend. In his complaint to Mark on their walk to the barns one day, this generous, competent, kindly old man sounds rather foolish: the "home material of Virginia was never so good," he says, "as when her roads were at their worst" (72–73). Littleton offers no rejoinder, the author no aside. Frank's statement is let to fall of its own weight when Isaac Tracy's rural peccadillo over some worthless land is revealed.

Isaac's only intellectual concern is a legal one. He is even more parochial than Meriwether. Reduced to idle cantankerousness on his rural estate, Tracy is nevertheless a veteran of the Revolutionary War and a careful farmer. He is a summing up, actually, of that good "home material of Virginia," produced in a bygone era, of which Meriwether has boasted. With nothing to divert him beyond the confines of his land, Tracy has evolved into a single-minded old crank who is more pathetic than comic in his intellectual emptiness. For years he and Meriwether have been in more or less friendly litigation over the ownership of a worthless piece of swampland that lies between their properties. When Meriwether contrives to end the suit in the old veteran's favor, Isaac Tracy is crestfallen. Suddenly he is left with nothing to occupy his mind in his rural retreat. He is portrayed as lost and confused as he "thought sorrowfully over the extinguished controversy. A favorite fancy had been annihilated, untimely cropped, as a flower of the field. He could not realize the idea. The privation left him no substitute" (322). His sense of loss will probably cause him to decline into lassitude, ill health, and boredom. At any rate, in his sojourner's overdone, melodramatic description of the old warrior's perplexity over so slight an affair, Kennedy enjoys some ironic laughter at Tracy's expense and demolishes Frank Meriwether's pride in the human products of the southern past.

Something languid, overly self-indulgent, and even decadent in the inhabitants of Swallow Barn finds a parallel at times in Littleton's landscape descriptions. The drowsy riverside landing he pictures after a Fourth of July outing is idyllically calm and appealing on one level. It is also a stultifying emblem of rural stasis and isolation, heavy and lifeless like the atmosphere before a thunderstorm:

> that striking repose, which is peculiar to the tide-water views; soft, indolent and clear, as if nature had retreated into this drowsy nook, and fallen asleep over her own image, as it was reflected from this beautiful mirror. The river was upwards of a mile in width, and upon its bosom were seen, for many a rood below, those alternate streaks of light and shade that are said to point out the channel, where its smooth surface was only ruffled by the frequent but lonely leap of some small fish above the water. A few shallops were hauled up on the beach, where some fishing-nets were stretched upon stakes. . . . Far below, and seemingly suspended in air amongst the brilliant reflections of the heavens, lay a small schooner at anchor, fixed as by a spell, and, nevertheless, communicating a sense of animation to this tranquil world by its association with beings that trod its noiseless deck. (160–61)

There is something wrong in the imagery here of narcissistic nature "fallen asleep over her own image," and in the noiseless "suspended in air" movements of those ghostly, dehumanized "beings," the sailors aboard the little schooner. These are all bucolic elements frozen in sunlight, like the magical forms of Seclusaval or Arnheim.

As usual in the pattern of antebellum pastoral, nature in *Swallow Barn* also reveals its bluntly terrifying other side. Goblin Swamp, through which Mark and Ned take an evening walk, assumes emblematic significance for the romance in its distortion of pastoral imagery, its gothic inversion of idyll. In the pastoral tradition, Ettin points out, the descent of evening is always ominous with a sense of "encroaching doom and unfolding danger."[8] As the two young men walk,

8. Ettin, *Literature and the Pastoral*, 136.

"distorted shadows fell through every weed, bush, and tree, and contributed, with the forlorn aspect of the landscape, to impress us with an undefined and solemn sensation, that for a moment threw us into silence" (250). As night deepens, great swamp trees are captured "in lurid shade" as a "chilling vapor" rises from the oozing marsh. John Davis's bird of ill omen, the hawk, darts up "with a hoarse scream into this fading light," and frogs and whippoorwills reiterate melancholy cries: "The foxfire,—as the country people call it,—glowed hideously from the cold and matted bosom of the marsh; and, far from us, in the depths of darkness, the screech-owl sat upon his perch, brooding over the slimy pool, and whooping out a dismal curfew, that fell upon the air like the cries of a tortured ghost" (260–61).

Having taken his bucolic ease and contemplated the human peculiarities induced by isolation and apparent security at Swallow Barn, Mark Littleton is quite ready and even glad to return to the active life of the city. His anticipation of his release from the plantation's deadening pastoral entrapment elicits those thoughts of "pleasant prospects" toward which his mind turns at the end of the romance. Mark admits here that the dream he tried to fulfill at Swallow Barn of "calm and dignified retirement of the woods" had only been a "very philosophical longing." There was nothing really serious about his trip into the *locus amoenus,* and so he feels no disappointment at what he has experienced of the barrenness of life there. He is simply eager to get away from the idle, petty, ill-fated place and its soporific, self-absorbed landscape. He actually has to laugh at his misdirected pastoral urge: "I begin to grow moderate in my desires; that is, I only want a thousand acres of good land, an old manor-house, on a pleasant site, a hundred negroes, a large library, a host of friends, and a reserve of a few thousands a year in the stocks,—in case of bad crops,—and, finally, a house full of pretty, intelligent, and docile children, with some few et ceteras not worth mentioning" (311).

Mark wants quite a bit. He is exaggerating, of course, making fun of himself and the hollow pride of the southern landed gentry. In the "feudal munificence" (71) of the plantation, as he referred to it earlier in the story, "I doubt not, after

this, I shall be considered a man of few wants, and great resources within myself" (311). Would that Isaac Tracy displayed some inner resource besides a commitment to petulant
litigation; or Ned and Bel something beyond their frenetic,
jejune pursuit of entertainment; or Frank Meriwether something more than his futile longing for life in a bygone Virginia. And Mark's practical wish, were he a planter, to have
reserve money in a bank also can puncture for the careful
reader any illusion of true self-sufficiency on a farm that Kennedy might accidentally have set up in his essentially ironic
depiction of life and death at Swallow Barn. By keeping his
contacts with Meriwether's despised outside world, as Virgil's
wise survivor Tityrus maintained his, Mark the imaginary
good shepherd in the idyllic environment is able to protect
his well-being, his family, and his possessions.

The "Pleasant Prospects" to which Mark Littleton refers in
the title of his last chapter certainly have nothing to do with
grateful recollections of the bucolic vagaries of Swallow Barn,
or a wish ever to return. He is referring to a glance outward
into the enfolding, protective city. Thoughts of home now re-
fresh his spirits, he comments to himself while packing, just
as the rainfall of the day and night before has renovated the
earth and the air (502). At the end of the romance, Mark
Littleton turns with relief to the real and busy world out
there. He turns away from the stifling insularity of southern
rural life where the ruling class is lulled into "certain fixed-
ness" of habits—he and Kennedy mean stubbornness—that
"even reject many of the valuable improvements of the day,"
such as good roads, for one thing, of which Kennedy himself
approved (71). Mark's rejection of the country life at Swallow
Barn is a unique turn in antebellum southern pastoral. *Swallow Barn* is a strange pastoral in reverse, where the idyllic vision is undercut by the author's intent to posit its opposite. As
in James Dickey's *Deliverance,* in *Swallow Barn* the city becomes the secure, desirable place. It becomes an urban *locus
amoenus* that offers the sojourner in the garden an image of
salubrious human activity and refuge to counterbalance the
lethargic, progress-denying life in fiction of southern plantation idyll.

The more traditional pastoral urge that occurs in antebellum romance is evident once more, though, in Kennedy's change of attitude in *Horse-Shoe Robinson*. In authorial asides here he sounds as backward-looking and nostalgic as Frank Meriwether. It is a recurrence of pastoral dilemma when Kennedy expresses preference for the social and moral values linked to a more bucolic way of life in a pre–Revolutionary War America locked dead in history, and evoked now and then by some idyllic imagery in his tale. By the time *Horse-Shoe Robinson* was published not long after *Swallow Barn*, Kennedy had become deeply concerned over what appeared to him to be the nation's tradition-denying, rootless future as a coldly commercial, crassly materialistic, and crudely industrial land devoid of monuments and memory. His moments of despondency brought on by a nagging—even maudlin, I think—awareness of the roguery and iniquity of the world were exacerbated, again, by what he saw as the flawed economies and class-conscious mob appeal resulting from Andrew Jackson's presidency, which he had supported wholeheartedly at first.[9] *Horse-Shoe Robinson* is set securely years in the past, during the Revolution. Its action starts when Major Arthur Butler undertakes a journey south from Virginia guided by Galbraith "Horse-Shoe" Robinson. Their goal is to join the American General Gates in the Carolinas for what was to be the Battle of King's Mountain.

Galbraith Robinson is another antebellum shepherd-frontiersman who this time has given up forest life for the settled trade of blacksmith, from which he derives his nickname. Typical of the frontiersman of southern romance, he is strong, truthful, modest, and capable. As usual he possesses "real delicacy of mind that lies at bottom of a kind nature," and a sturdy blue-eyed glance of "shrewd, homely wisdom."[10] Like his prototype, Davis's John Smith, he is the shepherd-rescuer because the not-too-competent Major Butler spends

    9. Bohner, *John Pendleton Kennedy*, 62–63.
    10. John Pendleton Kennedy, *Horse-Shoe Robinson: A Tale of the Tory Ascendency* (1852; rpr. ed. Ernest E. Leisy, New York, 1937), 9, 18, 55. All references to the work will be taken from this edition and noted parenthetically by page number in the text.

most of the romance out of the way as a prisoner of Tory partisans. He manages to escape once but is quickly recaptured.
Horse-Shoe finally rescues him in time to join the American
victory at King's Mountain. There Butler is reunited with his
secret wife Mildred Lindsay, daughter of British sympathizer
Philip, who owns a peculiar, isolated mountain-top retreat
called Dove Cote. With the battlefield reunion of the lovers,
Kennedy abruptly ends his story, as if he had suddenly grown
tired of it. Perhaps he was bothered with the hindsight that
the historical confrontation of armies he had chosen to describe was simply another unavoidable step in the loss of the
way of life he preferred in pre-Revolutionary America.

True to pastoral form death stalks the idyllic oases in *Horse-
Shoe Robinson*. They are not only threatened by a busy, war-
ring world outside, they also are destroyed by it. Bridges to
the past, strange to say, are all burned in the romance, except
for one ugly squatter-style subsistence farm that is far from
any ideal of country life. Kennedy's creative insight into truth
ultimately compels him to show that he knew better than se-
riously to propose even in fiction a possibility of regrasping
the past. Nevertheless, he yearned for it—hence, his bitterness.
The ruined rural retreats and farms in *Horse-Shoe Robinson*
are his unhappy metaphors for the damage to older, satisfac-
tory bucolic ways of life caused by the "mischievous inter-
polation" (15) of a new, crass, commercial and egalitarian
ethic in the post-Jacksonian nation.

Philip Lindsay's Dove Cote retreat seems safe enough on
its mountain near Charlottesville. It is a bit too secluded
and obsessively trim, though, like Seclusaval. As a metaphor
for a way of American life, it is at one unacceptable end
of Kennedy's depiction of rural existence in the romance.
Mildred calls Dove Cote a "little asylum" where her scholarly
father can study the supernatural, as he is wont to do, while
remaining "undisturbed by the angry passions of man" (120).
He sounds like Ruffner's Garame or Poe's Ellison. One silvery,
fantastically cloudy night Philip actually thinks he sees the
ghost of his deceased wife cross the garden. Her legacy is the
overly cultivated domain she planned for their retirement

from the threatening world. At the Cote clipped trees, graveled geometric walks, flower beds, pale statuary, and trimmed lawns all "evinced the dominion which a refined art may exercise with advantage over nature" (83, 90–91). In this strained, shudder-evoking pastoral environment so reminiscent of Seclusaval and Arnheim, Philip nearly goes out of his mind. So Kennedy is hardly serious when he describes this false *locus amoenus* as a place where a philosopher or a wearied statesman can relax and regain his thoughts (95). Only unnerving thoughts of the dead come to Philip, brooding over his mountain view. The war finally comes as well when the British Captain St. Jermyn arrives and lures him into open support of the English cause. The gardens and walks of Dove Cote are left to neglect and the return of the wilderness as St. Jermyn leads Lindsay to his death at King's Mountain while trying to guide him through the battle lines.

Allen Musgrove's North Carolina farm, on the other hand, is Kennedy's ideal pastoral place in *Horse-Shoe Robinson*. In it he fulfills his wish by creating an image of the Jeffersonian middle ground: the prosperous working farm tucked among trees and watered by a glistening river. It has all the pastoral ingredients attached to it including, naturally, vulnerability. The destructive forces from outside the idyll come in as Tories, whose warlike activities overwhelm the pastoral sounds of Musgrove's mill and lowing animals. The farm is burned to the ground, and the ideal it represents is lost to time and history (221, 326).

Wat Adair's badly tilled, scruffy mountain farm endures. It is at the other unacceptable end of Kennedy's rural places in the romance, a monument to bad farming and contempt for the nurturing land. Wat's settlement is a realistically described ramshackle collection of log cabins, shaggy fields of corn, rotting stumps, and clumsy pole fences. Worst of all is the surrounding blight of girdled trees. Echoing Paulding's complaint in *Westward Ho!*, Kennedy calls this scene a "field of the dead." There is no gothic affectation in his description of it. He is not having fun here inverting traditional pastoral imagery; he is graphically serious in his picture of a landscape ravaged through rapacity and neglect, the norm rather than the exception in southern agriculture of his day and before. Adair's trees

> had been death-stricken by the axe, and now heaved up their withered and sapless branches towards the heavens, without leaf or spray. In the phrase of the woodman, they had been girdled some years before, and were destined to await the slow decay of time in their upright attitude. It was a grove of huge skeletons that had already been bleached into an ashy hue by the sun, and whose stiff and dry members rattled in the breeze with a preternatural harshness. . . . It was a field of the dead; and the more striking in its imagery from the contrast which it furnished to the rich, verdurous, and lively forest that, with all the joyousness of health, encompassed this blighted spot. Its aspect was one of unpleasant desolation. (137–38)

Wat's desolate farm is a fitting emblem for the general wasting of values and order Kennedy felt the "mischievous interpolations" of change had brought upon post-Revolutionary America. A national "pernicious love of change," he laments in another authorial aside in *Horse-Shoe Robinson*, has obliterated so many "ancient associations" and "landmarks" as to make the country virtually rudderless (487). The "contentious crowd," the "wagoner's whip, the rude song of the boatman, and the clatter of the mill" are all part of the disturbing "hum of industry" that has disrupted the nation's ancient bucolic tranquility and sense of republican direction (15, 39). Frank Meriwether would have to agree.

There is further revelation of Kennedy's post–*Swallow Barn* pessimism and dilemma in a gloomy comment he gives Philip Lindsay before his death. The statement shows a sudden misanthropy, like Paulding's flash of bitterness against humanity in *The Backswoodsman*. To Mildred and his young son Henry, Philip complains that "God has given us a beautiful heaven, my children, and a rich and bountiful earth. He has filled both with blessings. Man only mars them with his cursed passions" (346). Unlike Paulding, however, Kennedy does not look to the contemporary Southwest for a fresh start for Americans. Instead, he wants to retrieve something out of the eighteenth century. For Kennedy and other malcontents of his time and place, the previous century represented a stage in national development that, to paraphrase Leo Marx, was more innocent and simpler than the present because its ideals were rooted in sound rural virtues.[11]

Horse-Shoe Robinson has none of the gentle good humor or subtle social criticism of *Swallow Barn*. Kennedy does nothing to hide his disgust with his era, but his barbs are general, not local. Before the Revolution, he goes on to say, "the great Western wilderness smiled with the contentment of a refined and polished civilization, which no after day in the history of this empire has yet surpassed—perhaps not equaled" (84). When he describes a force of frontiersmen hurrying to join battle against Cornwallis in North Carolina, Kennedy praises their rugged country hunting shirts and the hearty outdoor, independent spirit such simple, practical dress represents, which the "foppery of modern times has been allowed to displace" (499). After the quiet praise he gives progress in *Swallow Barn*, it is surprising to hear John Pendleton Kennedy sound like an antebellum Miniver Cheevy. There surely are times in *Horse-Shoe Robinson* when he does.

Having seen to the wreckage of his two pastoral places, the sterile parklike idyll of Dove Cote and the healthfully ideal working farm of Allen Musgrove, Kennedy quickly terminates his romance on a battlefield. The demons of time and change have triumphed in his Christian pastorals of death. He cannot prevent the destructive course of history even in his fiction. His great symbol or emblem for the loss of the good old ways in nineteenth-century American life is Wat Adair's hideous farm. It is a careless, rapacious gash in the forest, an affront to aesthetic values and productive husbandry. Adair's place is Kennedy's ironic *locus amoenus* that endures in *Horse-Shoe Robinson*, as does Mark Littleton's city in *Swallow Barn*.

11. Marx, *The Machine in the Garden*, 141.

5

William Alexander Caruthers and the Valley of Virginia

When William Alexander Caruthers commented in his own fiction on his troubled, changeful times, in *The Kentuckian in New York* (1834), he took grateful imaginative refuge in a southern idyll on a Virginia farm. Later, Simms's yearning compelled him to resort to picturing a similarly localized pastoral place in his romances, as Cooke also did in his. As can be expected in the antebellum southern fiction I am discussing, the *locus amoenus* in the romances of these three authors combines realistic regional details with classical Theocritan-Virgilian pastoral elements to provide a means for disguised social criticism and quietly expressed personal disappointment. Such disappointment is evident especially in Caruthers's next romance, *The Knights of the Golden Horse-Shoe* (1841), where he does not even allow himself in fiction the solace of attaining a secure idyllic place of retreat from the world. The paradisiacal *locus amoenus* toward which the action in this adventure heads is the mountain-locked vastness of the valley of Virginia, revealed in its pristine arcadian beauty and innocence for a moment of wonder, and then quickly destroyed by the pressing American realities of progress and development, again symbolized by the tree-felling axe. Caruthers was born in this valley, where the prosperous farms were small and well tended by so-called yeomen-farmers. Slaves were few here and posed no immediate threat or shame. As an adult, Caruthers established a successful medical practice far away in the Tidewater at Savannah, Georgia.

The Kentuckian in New York is a gentlemanly effort in epistolary form to create better understanding and toleration be-

tween North and South in a time of growing sectionalism in
the United States. It is the first American romance of any importance to deal with this national crisis, as Arthur Hobson
Quinn has noted.[1] The South was growing particularly irate
and secluded in its defiant, impatient responses to often ill-
informed and equally self-righteous northern Abolitionist attacks on its slave economy and mores. Caruthers's work,
though, is more than a mere polemic of exculpation. Because
of the easy informality of its imaginary letters and the realism
of their details of city and plantation life in the 1830s, the book
is not hard to read even today. In it Caruthers tries to describe
social shortcomings mainly pertaining to labor practices in
each section of the country. The letters are exchanged between
Victor Chevillere of Belville plantation on South Carolina's
Santee River and his college friend Beverley Randolph from
the idyllic farm in the valley of Virginia, who is visiting Belville while Victor is away on a trip to New York. At the plantation, Beverley observes and reports life to Chevillere, and falls
in love with his absent host's cousin Virginia Bell. On the
road North, Victor and his companion Augustus Lamar meet
Frances St. Clair, who is returning to her home in New York
after a holiday in the South. Victor falls in love with her, and
reports to Beverley what he sees on his trip.

   In the carriage they meet the Kentuckian of the title, Montgomery Damon, who is going to New York as well. Although
his outdoorsman's character places him in the tradition of the
courageous, chivalrous frontiersman figure in antebellum romance—he defends a lady at a New York circus by fighting and
whipping two city fops who have insulted her—Damon is
much modified.[2] For one thing he is married, for another he
wears homespun, and he is not a guide into the wilderness but
a tourist into the city like the others. He is a drover of cattle
and not a hunter (I, 19). The aristocratic southerners make him
one of their party along with Frances because they share a

   1. Arthur Hobson Quinn, *American Fiction: An Historical and Critical Survey* (New York, 1964), 113.
   2. Caruthers, *The Kentuckian in New York*, I,65–66. All references to the
work will be taken from this edition and noted parenthetically by volume
and page number in the text.

"sincere respect" for his "unsophisticated honesty" (I, 40). So in his way Caruthers idealizes Montgomery Damon as one of those frank, natural "yeomen of the west" (I, 73, 78), in whom Vernon Louis Parrington has said Caruthers placed his chief hope for the nation's harmonious progress and survival.[3]

Caruthers's point in *The Kentuckian in New York* is like Paulding's in *Letters from the South* and *Westward Ho!* Caruthers also advances the notion of the redemptive power of the West or Southwest, only with the whimsical addition that national salvation must come about by a miraculous reverse migration of values. Victor writes to Beverley that the confident and open spirit of the West must move to the East to revitalize the urban or plantation-bound, suspicious, jaded people of the seaboard. After such a happening, rivals in the North and South could meet freely on a neutral ground such as Baltimore and frankly "learn to estimate each other's good qualities, and bury or forget those errors which are inescapable from humanity" (I, 54).

As the travelers' adventures begin in *The Kentuckian in New York*, Victor Chevillere expresses regret at leaving what he perceives as the "quiet and pastoral scenes" of Belville. Beverley Randolph will disabuse him of this delusion in his letters. On the road northward, Victor experiences a growing melancholy and premonition of evil while hurrying commercial traffic on the road and a smoking horizon ahead mar his approach to Baltimore (I, 32–33). Later in New York, Damon cannot wait to get back to the clean "open forest ranges" and hunting diversions of Kentucky (II, 107). The social and cultural fakery of the city are exemplified for him in the theater. One night at a play, as Chevillere writes to Randolph, Damon blurted out: "'Why, here it's all make-believe; it's all sham; but out in old Kentucky we *have* the real things which you only pretend here; like we do scarecrows in a corn field'" (II, 108). Victor observes that the poor of the city are all too often unsuspecting country people who have been lured by the false promise of urban wealth and success. As economic failures they live in squalor, constituting the "lowest depths of human

---

3. Parrington, *The Romantic Revolution in America*, 44.

degradation and misery" in the shadows of fine business house façades (II, 28–30). But Caruthers does try to balance his criticism. He is quick, for instance, to mention the unhealthfulness of the plantation after his description of the sickly city. If the oppressed masses of the North are subject on top of everything else to plague in the summer heat, enslaved blacks, miserable poor whites, and even aristocrats like Beverley Randolph in the Belville mansion are susceptible to malaria. Beverley writes of getting ill, but most terrifying of all is his account of almost being murdered by a slave.

His experiences reveal that the Tidewater plantation's pleasant groves, flower-perfumed air, and docile pigeons flying over "garden and cotton fields" (I, 111, 118) are as much a sham as the fancy architecture and theater of the city. There is real terror in this southern garden, and the shudder of its recognition is a much more serious matter by far than the more or less playful literary shudders evoked by twisted pastoral imagery in "Seclusaval" or *Swallow Barn*. What troubles Randolph are Belville's uncommunicative slaves and their brutal black driver. Visiting the slave quarters in moonlight, he writes Chevillere how he felt as if he had been transported to another dark, threatening world, "into the center of Africa at once." There the "unsteady light of the pine logs before the door" of a cabin cast a "fitfull gleam of light upon some of these natives of the shores of the Niger, with their tatooed visages, ivory teeth, flat noses, and yellow blood-shot eyeballs" (I, 117–19). The shudder here derives from Caruthers's allusion to a deep-seated fear in the Old South of servile insurrection. This dread had been exacerbated only a couple of years before the publication of *The Kentuckian in New York* by Nat Turner's failed but bloody slave revolt near Norfolk, Virginia. The dissatisfied driver at Belville tries to kill Randolph by attempting to burn down the library where the visitor is dozing. Even though another slave foils the driver, Randolph describes the event to Victor as a "gloomy foreboding of the future" as he conjures up the southerners' nightmare vision of Abolitionist-stirred "outrages and uncontrollable fury of the savage mob" once the blacks are let loose (II, 71–72).

Just before he makes his terrifying visit to the slave quarters, however, Beverley's mind strays to the degrading use in the North of steam power. Where the dehumanization of labor is concerned in this romance of sectional healing, Caruthers of course does not want the South to come in for all the blame. The association of ideas he suggests through Randolph's reflection works like this: if the institution of agricultural slavery has created a sullen, degraded, potentially dangerous class of blacks in the South, so the institution of industrial labor has created a similarly unhappy, debased, rebellious subclass among whites in the North. In this long letter about types of slaves in America, Randolph first comments on how machinery has brought humanity into today's "mongrel age," where chivalry and romance are overwhelmed by the impersonal imperatives of steam power. The hero of the new industrial era, he writes, operates a steam-driven spinning jenny and "sings doggerel to the music of the hand organ" powered by the same source (I, 114). Thus Caruthers introduces his readers to the southern quarters by way of the northern factory.

His seemingly careful balance of problems North and South has already tipped, though, in favor of the latter in Frances St. Clair's comparison of the Hudson River mountain scenery to the southern Blue Ridge she had recently seen. Walking with Victor she tells him, as he informs Randolph, that the southern mountains are more restful than these "highlands of the Hudson," where "there is such a stir of busy life, such an atmosphere of steam, and clouds of canvas, that one is perpetually called back in spirit to the stir and bustle of city life." In the Blue Ridge, on the other hand, there is no evidence of the city's busy commercial pace, and "primitive nature seems to have returned upon us with all its balmy delights—quiet and peacefulness" (I, 49). For all Caruthers's sincere desire to encourage amelioration of the nation's sectional rift, the southern antebellum romancers' typical pastoral preference to withdraw to an imaginary idyll surfaces at the end of his story, with all its local bias and futile resistance to change.

Located in the mountain-enclosed valley of Virginia far from machines and plantations, urban and rural slaves, and physical and spiritual poverty, the pleasant country place in

The Kentuckian in New York hints at Caruthers's weariness with the stressful outside world and the hopeless task he had set himself in his fiction. His facile comparison of black chattel slavery in the South to white industrial slavery in the North, after all, is only another presentation of the old argument used easily and often by apologists for the South's peculiar institution. Amelioration in his book resolves itself into an image of antebellum southern peace and harmony in an isolated *locus amoenus* that rejects both the city and the plantation for a Jeffersonian alternative to industrial development and feudal estates. Montgomery Damon returns to Kentucky; Victor Chevillere, Frances St. Clair, and Augustus Lamar head for Virginia, where Beverley Randolph will meet them at his farm with Virginia Bell.

Having attained the crest of the Blue Ridge Mountains on his way home, Beverley looks east behind him. There, as he writes in his last letter to Victor, he sees "dilapidated houses, and overgrown fields, and all the evidences of a desperate struggle with circumstances far beyond their control." Ahead, west in the valley of Virginia he sees the restful idyll that lies at the critical core of antebellum romance: "On the western side . . . a long and happy valley stretches far as the eye can reach, with its green hills and cultivated vales, neat farmhouses, and fragrant meadows, and crystal springs, and sparkling streams, its prosperous villages, its numerous churches, and schools, and happy, happy people" (II, 193–94).

It is near Christmas when the travelers reunite at Beverley's farm for marriage to their respective fiancées. This rural place is located suitably so as to keep away the "fierce struggles of the world." It is a bucolic retreat, nevertheless, that is less static than usual in antebellum romance. There is the excellent descriptive touch Caruthers adds, for example, of fall leaves rippling across the lawn. Natural auditory imagery is important as well in giving life and conviction to the scene. Caruthers is at pains to soothe his readers' troublesome recollections of town and Tidewater, especially thoughts of those brooding, ungenial slaves at Belville:

> The sun was just sinking in the western horizon, behind a long veil
> of fleecy and dappled winter clouds, tinged with the richest hues

of crimson and pink; a gentle breeze was just rippling the red and dried-up leaves along the lawn, and monotonously sounded through the naked boughs of the grove of ancient oaks, which stood around and in front of the venerable domicile of the Randolphs; the hounds had sought the protection of the kennel from the chills of the evening, and the solitary bell of the ancient wether, as he led the little flock into the primitive-looking fold, could just be heard above the lowing of the few household cattle which still remained unsheltered; all external objects around the venerable establishment bore that delightful aspect of rural repose which is so soothing to those who yet retain, after the fierce struggles of the world, a heart susceptible of these simple emotions, and a conscience untainted by crime. (II, 200)

If it had been left up to Governor Spotswood, as Caruthers fictionalizes him with great poetic license in *The Knights of the Golden Horse-Shoe*, Virginia's valley would not have been developed even to the Jeffersonian stage of idyllic perfection of the Randolph farm. In *Southward Ho! A Spell of Sunshine*, William Gilmore Simms in the mid-1850s called the part of the valley where the Shenandoah River flows a "most perfect idea of Arcadia . . . a dream of peace sheltered by the wings of security." The valley in *The Knights of the Golden Horse-Shoe* represents the same thing for Caruthers, a pastoral "garden spot of the land."[4] The noble, doomed Shawnee chief Chunoluskee describes the valley in this romance using words so enticing that they could have come from an account of one of those first ecstatic English travelers to Virginia's shores: "It is the most glorious land that ever the sun shone upon, there is a valley beyond those mountains, almost a perfect terrestrial paradise, abounding in deer, elk, buffalo, and game of every sort—the land teeming with wild fruits of every kind, and bright with purest fountains of water that ever gushed from the solid rocks" (57).

With such an idealized picture of the interior to spur him

---

4. William Gilmore Simms, *Southward Ho! A Spell of Sunshine* (New York, 1854), 178; William Alexander Caruthers, *The Knights of the Golden Horse-Shoe: A Traditionary Tale of the Cocked Hat Gentry* (1845; rpr. with introduction by Curtis Carroll Davis, Chapel Hill, 1970), 27. All references to the work will be taken from this edition and noted parenthetically by page number in the text.

on, Spotswood's exploration gets under way after some slowly paced opening chapters involving the disguise and exoneration of the young protagonist Frank Lee. Accused in England of complicity in Prince Charles's effort to seize the crown in 1745, Lee has fled to Spotswood's Temple Farm in the guise of a tutor named Harry Hall. In Virginia he is accused of murdering John Spotswood, the governor's drunken son who has seduced the Indian beauty Wingina. (Caruthers has taken one of the "justifiable liberties of fiction" he refers to in the introduction to the first edition of his romance in providing the historical bachelor Spotswood with a wife and four children.) Wingina is Chunoluskee's sister, and both were educated at William and Mary. At Lee's trial she confesses that her brother killed John. Frank is cleared, sheds his disguise, and joins Spotswood's Tramontine Expedition to the Blue Ridge Mountains. The bulk of the narrative concerns this exploration, and the consequent incremental, ironic loss of yet another American Eden.

Governor Spotswood and the frontiersman-guide Joe "Red" Jarvis are the best-drawn characters in the romance. The ease of manner with which Caruthers generally handles the scenes in which they appear breathes some life into the otherwise high-flown, turgid diction of the story. Caruthers certainly is not as relaxed or as amiable in *The Knights of the Golden Horse-Shoe* as he was in *The Kentuckian in New York*. No doubt his likening of the Valley of Virginia to Eden's "terrestrial paradise" gave him a share of the somber thoughts of cosmic loss that accompany the image. A consciousness, then, of the greater weightiness of his theme in *The Knights of the Golden Horse-Shoe* might be reflected in the high style of the narrative—this and the requisite verbal posturing that his time demanded to give respectability to the crafting and reading of fiction. So it is that Chunoluskee and Spotswood both are given speeches whose descriptions of the land are imbued with Judaeo-Christian biblical imagery. When speaking to the House of Burgesses in an effort to raise funds for his expedition, Spotswood seems to be making a prophecy about Canaan: "Behold the rich meadows, and neat farm houses, and the gilded spires as they point toward heaven" (123).

He gets his money, and also the respect and devotion of the woodsman Jarvis, who calls him a "tip, top old feller, in the field" (197). The governor's practical side that appealed to Jarvis is evident in his dress. He is first seen in the accouterments of a gentleman-hunter seated on the veranda of his rambling mansion. He wears a hunting shirt; his feet with their gaitered legs rest on the railing; his hunting gun leans ready in a nearby corner as his dog sleeps at the base of his chair (2). In appearance as well as in oratorical ability, honesty, and sentimentality, he is a nineteenth-century version in period costume of John Donald Wade's Cousin Lucius in *I'll Take My Stand*.

Typical of his kind in antebellum southern romance, Joe Jarvis, the hunter, Indian fighter, and scout, exudes the self-confidence of having survived the rigors of life in the outdoors. His face is full of "fun and frolic" of "a quiet and subdued sort" (175). As Spotswood's army of exploration starts out of Williamsburg, Joe cannot resist a wry comment to the governor on the inappropriate elegance of the dress of the young cavaliers who are among the ranks of foresters and yeoman militia. "Why I was thinkin', Sir," he says, "how all this gold and flummery would look the day we marched in again" (176). Later and more tongue-in-cheek he advises Spotswood to turn the festive excursion into a "great hunting party" (181). As the guide of civilization into the wilderness, Jarvis teaches Frank Lee how to survive by hunting in the forest. In further jeering reference to Spotswood's card-playing, wine-drinking, cock-fighting young followers, he says to Frank, "You'll see who's the best man among us, when we get among the mountains, and when neither money nor larnin' can do much for a man" (185–86).

Frank helps Jarvis as frontiersman-shepherd to blaze a trail toward the Blue Ridge, and to guard the camp against Indians at night. There is a settled side to Jarvis also that recalls Horse-Shoe Robinson and Montgomery Damon. When the horses of the expedition begin to give out because their hooves used to the soft Tidewater earth cannot stand the increasingly rocky terrain, Jarvis teaches Spotswood and his men how to make horseshoes. He had the foresight to bring farrier's equipment along with him, and he charges the cavaliers for his services (211–12). Although the action he takes at the story's conclusion strangely belies what he says here, there is pathos nonetheless in Jarvis's voice when he tells Frank one day that "I'm a hunter by trade, and settlements have been crowding on me for some time, and this here mountain scheme of the Governor's—though the old codgers laugh at it—is going to make things a heap worse with me" (185).

Dispossession is what Caruthers is writing about under the surface of his adventure romance. *The Knights of the Golden Horse-Shoe* is a chronicle of ruin, a tale of the movement of a debasing civilization westward into virgin land whose fresh hopefulness for humanity diminishes as the explorers cut their way through the forest to the incongruous but symbolically fitting sounds of drums and bugles. These, to Jarvis's disgust, chase the game away (195). Here is the cacophonic panoply of a war-making culture moving in upon another southern Eden:

> The white tents stretching out in picturesque lines against the fading green of the forest; the bright blaze of the camp fires, throwing fantastic shadows of the wagons and the horses, and moving objects around; the merry laugh of those within; the rude jest; the recounting of the adventures of the day; the loud song of the old soldiers of the life guard; the measured tramp of the sentinels on duty; the neighing of the horses in the forest, the braying of the asses and the mules; the lowing of cows . . . altogether present an enchanting scene amid the primeval forests of nature. (187–88)

At every encampment they make, young cavaliers and old guard game and drink and sing late into the night (196). Chunoluskee has fled into the forest ahead of the explorers to arouse the Indians against the white man's coming. With him he has taken kidnapped Wingina and a white girl named Egenia Elliot, whom Jarvis rescues at the end. As a result of Chunoluskee's machinations, a guard is tomahawked to death at the edge of camp one morning. In this way the killing on the road to Arcadia begins.

In tracing the laborious advance of Spotswood's men, Caruthers is making the familiar tragic point that underlies such antebellum southern romances: the more civilization en-croaches upon the gardenlike wilderness, the farther away the dream of American Arcadia withdraws. Complications of abduction, massacre, revenge, and hate ripple in and out of the expedition as it moves toward Virginia's valley. Chuno-luskee's description of a terrestrial paradise there becomes smothered in imagery of disharmony and war: "It was a gal-lant sight to behold that bright and joyous band of cavaliers, in their plumes and brilliant dresses and fluttering banners, not yet soiled by the dust and toil of travel, as they wound through the green vistas fresh from the hands of nature, and their prancing steeds still elastic and buoyant with high blood and breeding. It cheered the heart of the veteran warrior, their commander, to see the columns file off before him as he sat upon his horse and received their salutes" (205).

At the settlement of Germanna the explorers find more de-struction and death. The Indians have slaughtered and muti-lated the inhabitants and burned all the buildings. Jarvis is glad that Spotswood sees the unburied, horrible bodies; the hunter is eager for a battle with the Indians. On the night of another cockfight in camp, the natives attack. First they cause an avalanche of rocks among the once quiet, autumn trees. Then they light fires around the camp to burn out the white intruders, but the wind changes and turns the flames on the Indians, who flee. In the unnatural light of the fire the colonists see a strange image of the death of an imperial city, "spires and domes, and huge edifices, encircled with the flames" (222).

It is significant for understanding Caruthers's pastoral change of heart at the end of his romance that such a startling image of the ruin of cities should occur on the verge of Spots-wood's discovery of the valley—"this future seat of empires" (122), as he described it to the burgesses. There is a sympathy for nature lying behind Caruthers's fire imagery that would halt the development of the untouched land. At the crest of the Blue Ridge Mountains, on whose slopes the battle in the flames took place, the men of the Tramontine Expedition look down on a vast valley that seems "like a great sea of vegeta-tion in the moon-light, rising and falling in undulating and

picturesque lines" as far as the eye can see: "There lay the
Valley of Virginia . . . in its first freshness and purity . . . what
a solemn and sublime temple of nature was there" (229). By
the governor's order the Indians are exiled from their earthly
paradise. Jarvis asks permission to start clearing trees at once
for a settlement, but the awestruck Spotswood orders him to
wait. Having purged the land of its human inhabitants, he
hesitates to do anything more with it. The valley is now like
Eden was before Adam and Eve appeared, where "nature
in her primitive simplicity and purity reigns forever" (131,
241). When he rebels against the first cutting of Eden's de-
populated forests that Joe Jarvis is suddenly so eager to get on
with, the old governor sounds as fustily reactionary as Frank
Meriwether at Swallow Barn; and Caruthers reflects a misanthropy almost as weary as Paulding's in *The Backwoodsman* or Kennedy's in *Horse-Shoe Robinson*.

But Caruthers is very sure about his meaning, for Spotswood's yearning, wonder, and hesitation refer to a crucial
statement Frank Lee made much earlier in the story. His observation on the futility of humanity's dream of finding sur-
cease from struggle and sorrow in an idyllic garden is almost
lost in a long, soporific conversation he has with his beloved
Ellen Evylin, daughter of Spotswood's physician. Frank's
nearly hidden words clearly identify Caruthers's awareness of
the dark philosophical application of the pastoral imagery he
uses in his romances. With an unexpectedly world-weary unhappiness that undermines the optimism of Caruthers's tale
of the discovery of one more American Eden, Frank says to
Ellen that "the experience of our race seems to be everywhere
the same. Not only was it cursed and condemned to earn its
bread by the sweat of the brow, but the sentence extends
much farther. . . . We are just allowed to peep into the garden
of Eden, and then banished forever amidst the dark by-ways
and crowded thoroughfares of busy life" (96).

The entire adventure of *The Knights of the Golden Horse-
Shoe* works out this sentence—this theme of human banish-
ment from the garden, from Eden or Arcadia. The valley's Indians are brutally dispossessed of their ancestral paradisiacal
hunting grounds. There is not much tranquillity and joy in

the future for Caruthers's white men either. Spotswood seems stripped of his Cousin Lucius vitality and joie de vivre as he sees his dream of a terrestrial paradise on the other side of the mountains slip away. Time, change, and death move in on the southern idyll as the practical, restless, implacable Joe Jarvis begins wielding his axe in the "freshness and purity" of the newly discovered forests and meadows of the valley of Virginia in order to build a town.

6

William Gilmore Simms, the Serpent, and Captain Porgy

Of all these part-time gentlemen-authors of the Old South, William Gilmore Simms of Charleston, South Carolina, came closest to being a professional writer. As he declares in his preface to the 1855 edition of *Guy Rivers* (1834), the great popularity of the book, his second romance, made him decide to give up a career in politics to become a "novelist and romancer." He also was a magazine editor, essayist, and poet. Simms was a prolific writer. In letters, however, he more than once admitted to being careless and impatient in his work, and indifferent to revision. "I write like steam, recklessly, perhaps thoughtlessly," he told his friend James Lawson, the New York businessman and writer who was virtually Simms's literary agent in the northern city where his romances were published (Simms, *Letters*, I, 178; III, 11; V, 400).

Through marriage Simms was able to make his living as a planter at a time when southern writers would have starved if they had had to rely on local patronage. So Simms himself wrote with disgust in the February 1841 issue of *The Magnolia* magazine, less than a decade after the first flush of *Guy Rivers*. As a writer and intellectual in the antebellum South, he was not alone in feeling socially and psychologically like a "man apart," in Bertram Wyatt-Brown's words in *Southern Honor*. It is with surprising and revealing bitterness, for instance, that Henry Timrod, a local friend of Simms and one of the South's best poets, wrote in an article for *Russell's Magazine* of August 1859 that the southern author is the "Pariah of modern literature." A sense of dissociation and isolation weighed on Simms and other authors and thinkers of the Old South, linking them in this particular way at least to their northern counterparts who, Drew Gilpin Faust states in *A Sacred Circle*, associated their own regional neglect with a national loss of traditional values and a decline of gentility.[1]

Woven through Simms's romances, essays, and poems is a pessimism about the human experience and a criticism of American hyperactivity and restlessness that are deeper and more bitterly felt than any that appear in the work of his fellow regional writers. His dark critical view is the epitome of theirs. It coruscates throughout his fiction in pastoral contrasts where images of bucolic calm and beauty are set against or compromised by more frequent descriptions of bucolic ruin and ugliness. Writing on another occasion in 1841, Simms complained in *The Magnolia* of the American trait of restlessness and especially of haste to get things done, which gives a "lack of permanence, stability and finish to all that we undertake and all that we perform"—qualities that make us as a nation look "ridiculous" to boot (Simms, *Letters*, I, 224).

Two years before making this statement Simms had written James Kirke Paulding in praise of the kind of "mental restlessness" that keeps a nation strong. At the same time he condemned the typical American physical restlessness that simply "makes a nation unstable" (Simms, *Letters*, I, 144). Simms expresses this attitude even in his earliest extant letters, written in 1826 from the Mississippi frontier.[2] Nevertheless, Simms found it impossible to reconcile his forward-looking admiration for "Doing"—as he called the kind of positive political, social, and economic progress that he also often parochially associated with Yankees—with his reclusive urge toward sequestered security, permanence, and repose, as exemplified by his depiction of the agrarian southern *locus amoenus* in his romances. From this arises his particular pastoral dilemma. His pastoral yearning to get away from everyday life in his fiction is tied in, too, with his peculiar per-

1. William Gilmore Simms, "Southern Literature," *Magnolia*, III (February 1841), 69, 71; Bertram Wyatt-Brown, *Southern Honor: Ethics and Behavior in the Old South* (New York, 1982), 98; Henry Timrod, "Literature in the South," *Russell's Magazine*, V (August 1859), 385; Faust, *A Sacred Circle*, x–xi, 144–48.

2. James Everett Kibler, Jr., "The First Simms Letters: 'Letters from the West' (1826)," *Southern Literary Journal*, XIX (Spring 1987), 81–91.

sonal sense of suffering and sorrow. Simms felt marked by ill-fate.

Sometimes when he complains along these lines Simms sounds like an antebellum Job. At one point he writes James Lawson that in life "shipwreck and suffering are inevitable" (Simms, *Letters*, II, 456). He delights in "deep tragedy," he laments to Mrs. Sarah Hale, a Boston writer and editor. Simms professes to feel his share of such tragedy when in another letter he tells the South Carolina lawyer, educator, and politician William Porcher Miles that he knows himself to be marked by the scourge, "pursued by a hungry Fate . . . insatiate archer" (Simms, *Letters*, II, 560; IV, 400–402). As a culmination to this train of thought, in 1862 after a mysterious fire broke out in his plantation mansion at Woodlands (a second, quite unmysteriously caused by Sherman's soldiers, occurred in 1865 and resulted in a total loss of house and contents) Simms confides to the South Carolina politician and kindred intellectual James Henry Hammond that a "Fate has pursued me for more than thirty years of loss, trial, trouble, denial, death, destruction, in which youth has passed rapidly to age, and hope into resignation that is only not despondency. It is my chief consolation that I have been able to endure so well, and if the Fate smites, the God strengthens . . . I am patient" (Simms, *Letters*, IV, 403).

As a means, then, of giving some vent to his personal longings and anxieties, and of expressing dissatisfaction with national and regional affairs, Simms in all of his romances juxtaposes brief scenes of static, idyllic peace with longer scenes of action gone strangely, disastrously awry. In a pause in *The Partisan* (1835), for instance, he describes "Swamp Fox" Francis Marion's hard-riding Revolutionary War dragoons resting near a cool and tranquil roadside spring. Unexpectedly, Simms intrudes his own dejected voice into the narrative to muse how man invariably will reject the harmonies of "the bird and the flower," so bent is he "upon earthly strife," as symbolized by his story's great action of war.[3] Yet in *The*

---

3. William Gilmore Simms, *The Partisan: A Tale of the Revolution* (2 vols.; New York, 1835), II,261. All references to the work will be taken from this edition and noted parenthetically by volume and page number in the text.

Forayers (1855) Captain Porgy, Simms's comic relief and frequent philosophical spokesman, states in apparent contradiction to the green and sunlit changelessness of Simms's restful pastoral ideal: "It is stagnation that is death."[4]

Guy Rivers, the educated, doomed Georgia bandit leader, exemplifies Simms's view of humanity's destructive preference for busyness and strife to repose and contemplation. He is one of Simms's many memorable characters, and his criminal spirit dominates *Guy Rivers*, which takes place in the rugged, dangerous north Georgia gold fields of the early nineteenth century where Ruffner's garden builder Garame made his fortune. In this romance Rivers is the figurative "serpent"—that well-worn image from Genesis that Simms uses again and again for villains in his stories, with varying degrees of heavy-handed allusiveness. Much more important than this link to the archetypal pastoral counterforce, Satan, is the fact that Guy Rivers is the first Faust figure in southern fiction. Simms describes him as a man who had "that ambition of one who discovers at every step that nothing can be known, yet will not give up the unprofitable pursuit, because even while making the discovery, he still hopes vainly that he may yet, in his own person, give the maxim the lie . . . for ever battling and for ever lost."[5] In his nihilistic striving for knowledge and power in his dark forest cave and in the ferocious activity of his robberies and murders, Guy is the *reductio ad absurdum* of Simms's recurrent assertion that "Being is nothing without Doing" (Simms, *Letters*, III, 438)—a concept that persists as an uncomfortable companion to his pastoral longing.

Significant for the theme in *Guy Rivers* of the breaking down of human, particularly American and southern, aspirations, endeavors, and works is Guy's murder of Simms's first frontiersman. This idealized southerner, appropriately named Mark Forrester, is killed off early by Rivers when Forrester befriends Ralph Colleton, hero of the romance, after

4. Simms, *The Forayers*, 529.
5. William Gilmore Simms, *Guy Rivers: A Tale of Georgia* (2 vols.; New York, 1834), II,111. All references to the work will be taken from this edition and noted parenthetically by volume and page number in the text.

rescuing him from another of the outlaw's ambushes. Later Simms's woodsmen are more realistically drawn, such as John "Thumbscrew" Witherspoon of *Mellichampe* (1836) or Jim Ballou of *The Forayers* (1855) and *Eutaw* (1856). As is usual for his type of character in antebellum southern romance, Mark is handsome, strong, and agile; he is good-natured, of course, and self-controlled; his eye has a twinkle that promises good fellowship and a heart at ease. His features are "frank and fearless . . . finely southern," and lack the "calculating lines of cunning." The phrase "finely southern" is something new in the delineation of the shepherd-frontiersman in antebellum romance. Furthermore, Mark's spirit is of the kind that "at an earlier period of human history" begot the "practices of chivalry" (I, 52–57).

To Nathaniel Beverley Tucker, a law professor at William and Mary College and a fellow romancer, Simms wrote that his ideal in literature was to "write truthfully, honestly, and with out affection" (Simms, *Letters*, III, 11). Very often he succeeds in doing this. Even his idealized, specifically southern frontiersman-savior Mark Forrester is marred by a hot, excitable "restlessness" (I, 106). Driven by the great American flaw that ruins so many of Simms's characters and idyllic places, Mark has no patience to settle down as an honest farmer of the kind Simms glorifies along with "sacred" trees in a *Ladies' Companion* article of August 1841.[6] Like so many others at the Chestattee settlement described in *Guy Rivers*, Forrester wants to get rich quickly by digging for gold. Impatient greed drives him to join an illegal squatter mining operation that ends in a bloody crushing to death of state guardsmen who have been sent to stop the diggings on Indian land (I, 214–23). Forrester's remorse is terminated only when Guy Rivers kills him.

Guy's evil passions are the spiritual center of the blighted Georgia landscape Simms depicts in the romance, and its rootless, destructive settlers corrupted by the lust for gold. On Ralph Colleton's way from Tennessee to his home in South

6. William Gilmore Simms, "The Good Farmer," *Ladies' Companion*, XV (August 1841), 155, 157.

Carolina, where he is to marry his first cousin Ellen at the end of his adventures, Ralph enters a countryside whose hills and shaggy pines have a "dreary and melancholy expression, which cannot fail to elicit in the bosom . . . a feeling of gravity and even gloom" (I, 2). But this nonidyllic opening, symbolic as it is of Guy's spirit, is shortly balanced by a pastoral scene that is Simms's metaphor for something lovely and lost. The ugly Chestattee settlement Ralph enters is surrounded by beautiful virgin forests still "undishonored by the axe" (I, 59). Unlike Caruthers and Cooke, Simms never speaks disparagingly of steam power. For him, as for Paulding, the primitive axe is a major symbol of the despoliation of the land and of too-rapid, ill-conceived transition in the United States.

Busy Chestattee at midday is grimly realistic. Simms's prose is at its truthful best here, and his description is uncluttered, crisp, and perceptive. Chestattee is a place of rudely constructed houses, hacked and piled logs, rotting tree stumps, and dust. It is a boom town filled with the action and noise of hurrying, warlike, and greedy men. In the pattern that continues to develop in his romances after *Guy Rivers*, Simms first describes and then turns away from such uncongenial activity as he allows himself nostalgic lapses into pastoral reverie that are weighted with his own dissatisfied, painful, dreamy yearning.

At an outdoor Sunday service shortly after he has settled into Chestattee, Ralph imagines that the trees form a temple of leaves more perfect than any built by human hand. His mind turns to a mythical past, to a time of garden repose, away from the troubled Georgia gold fields. He looks back to an arcadian time when God was in the "trees, hills, and vales, the wild flowers and the murmuring water, all the work of his hands, attesting to his power, keeping their purpose." Ralph thinks of the "forms and features of that primitive worship, when a visible deity dwelt in the shadowed valleys, and whispered an auspicious acceptance of their devotions in every breeze" (I, 167).

Withdrawing in this way from the pervasive theme of action gone wrong, Simms betrays his pastoral urge and futile nostalgic preference for dead times in Greek myth or American history. As the frontier women start to sing hymns at the service, it becomes Simms's and not Ralph's voice that ruminates over how such "strains" must have been heard by the "old shepherds out among the hills, tending their charges" when God walked among them (I, 170). When word comes that the squatters have taken over the gold fields, Simms's pastoral reflections and longings suddenly disintegrate, as is typical of his pattern of writing. The outside world has intruded harshly to end the idyllic reverie.

Sadly, and in unmistakable conflict once again with the urge in his romances toward the pastoral ideal of peace, Simms writes in *Egeria* (1853), a catchall volume of commentary, that human passions must ever be Doing, for "man is no more made for solitude than sleep. . . . The repose of the passions must not imply their stagnation. They must rouse themselves at last and go forth, though it be only to bear a burden and be baffled by defeat. Successful or baffled, still the same— their deity is in the struggle. The struggle itself, is the life."[7] Simms's uncertain resignation to the need for human activity and Yankee-style business is reflected as well in something Captain Porgy says to a fellow guerrilla in *The Partisan:* "Our nature is never so legitimately employed . . . as when it is inventing, contriving, multiplying images and offices, the purposes and pleasures of which are to keep us from stagnation" (II, 89). This is a philosophy that Captain Porgy's actions deny later on in *Woodcraft* (1852).

The passions of the proud, ambitious, darkly beautiful, and unproductive poet Margaret Cooper of Kentucky are just so roused and "baffled by defeat." She is one of Simms's remarkable female creations—an Old South version in this case of Hawthorne's Zenobia of *The Blithedale Romance* (1852). "Fancy," Simms writes at the end of *Charlemont* (1856), "a confident country girl—supreme in her district over the Hobs and Hinnies—in conflict with the adroit man of the world, and you have the whole history of Margaret Cooper."[8] This ro-

7. William Gilmore Simms, *Egeria; or, Voices of Thought and Counsel, for the Woods and Wayside* (Philadelphia, 1853), 88–89.
8. William Gilmore Simms, *Charlemont; or, The Pride of the Village* (New York, 1856), 401. All references to the work will be taken from this edition and noted parenthetically by page number in the text.

mance and its sequel *Beauchampe* (1856), both reworked from an 1842 publication titled *Beauchampe*, are based on the so-called Kentucky Tragedy, a sordid real-life tale involving an upper-class seduction and murder in early nineteenth-century Lexington. *Charlemont* is heavily padded with self-conscious and pessimistic allusions to the Fall of Man in the Garden of Eden as retold by John Milton in *Paradise Lost.* Like Margaret, and like Eve, the inhabitants of the idyllic village Charlemont lacked the "all-in-all content," Simms writes at the beginning of *Beauchampe,* and so they lost their pastoral ease.[9] At the conclusion of the previous volume, *Charlemont,* Simms calls the seduction of rural Margaret by the city man Alfred Stevens the "triumph of the serpent" (400).

As *Charlemont* opens, Simms describes a bucolic ideal. Then he denies it in order to show what he felt was the final, tragic truth: humankind will lose the contentment of the Garden again and again because they are driven by the same demonic, restless spirit that ruins bestial Guy Rivers, gentlemanly Mark Forrester, and dreamy Margaret Cooper. Right or wrong, man is a Doer, Simms would say, who will always manage to wreck his earthly paradise. The real significance of *Charlemont,* though, lies in Simms's use of idyllic imagery as prophetic allegory of the doom of his agrarian South.

In the Charlemont community Simms creates another fleeting picture of his southern *locus amoenus.* On the whole it is an amplification of the pastoral vision in which he indulges in an authorial aside amid all the personal and social wreckage he describes in *Guy Rivers.* There, in the squalor of Chestattee, Simms sees for a fleeting moment the forlorn possibility of shady, flowery hamlets where society is "small and well intentioned," and the affections are won into "limpid and ever-living currents, touched for ever, here and there, by the sunshine, and sheltered in their reposes by overhanging leaves and flowers, for ever fertile and for ever fresh" (I, 264–65). This is Simms's later depiction of southern idyll in *Charlemont:* "In the winding hollows of those hills, beginning at our feet, you see the first signs of as lovely a little hamlet as ever

9. William Gilmore Simms, *Beauchampe; or, The Kentucky Tragedy* (1856; rpr. Chicago, 1890), 16.

promised peace to the weary and the discontented. . . . A dozen snug and smiling cottages seem to have been dropped in this natural cup, as if by magic" (18). "As if by magic" is as crucial a phrase for understanding here as it is in Ruffner's description of the impossible Seclusaval. Simms is only weaving a familiar spell in antebellum romance and toying with a favorite allusion.

Right after Simms describes the idyll of Charlemont, he points to its wreckage. An American Eden disappears even as Simms lets the reader glimpse it. The very next lines in the passage read: "The garden is no longer green with fruits and flowers—the festoons no longer grace the lowly portals—the white palings are down and blackening in the gloomy mould—the roofs have fallen, and silence dwells lonely among the ruins" (18). The neat counterbalancing of idyll and its antithesis in this description of the little village and its bucolic environment before and after the satanic Stevens comes reflects once more the essential irony of modern pastoral, where the ideal is linked to its opposite and thoughts of the Golden Age evoke thoughts of loss.

The hamlet of Charlemont falls into ruin after Margaret is corrupted by Stevens, who as pastoral counterforce has played upon his victim's vanity and boredom by promising to make her a great American poet. Themselves restless, and scandalized by Margaret's sin, the villagers leave their rural retreat. Margaret and her mother retire deeper into an uncongenial countryside to live out their days in a poor cottage. To lend the greatest moral weight and tragic dimension he can to his slight tale, Simms make this parallel clear: it was similar human vanity and desire for change that caused Eden to choke with weeds after Eve had given in to the wiles of Satan. Still, later in *Charlemont* the old teacher Mr. Calvert, who had left the village for advancement in the city where he failed as an attorney, praises discontent as the heart's hope to his friend Bill Hinkley, the good young man whose love Margaret rejected for Stevens's conniving flattery. Determined despite his ironic failure in the world outside the pastoral place, Calvert says that "doing is after all and before all, the great object of living" (151–52). He feels that the isolation of a village is morally debilitating for its inhabitants. Life in such a place is unreal and stultifying; in the end this is the cause of Margaret's unhappiness and pride.

Calvert's active philosophy of Doing and Charlemont's bucolic ruin reveal all over again Simms's recurring dilemma in reconciling action to rural calm in his romances. Well before Calvert gives his speech in the story, Simms criticizes Doing in one of his authorial asides. The discontent that is inherent in human activity is the national curse, he says. Charlemont, he speculates, was "most probably abandoned . . . in compliance with the feverish restlessness of mood—that sleepless discontent of temper, which, perhaps . . . is the moral failing of the Anglo-American" (19). The final truth that Simms gets out of his ideal hamlet is that humans, especially Americans, are never satisfied with what they have. The disastrous ambition of Margaret Cooper in particular makes this point.

Wrecked Charlemont on the Kentucky frontier is Simms's gloomy metaphor for both the missed Jeffersonian middle ground of farming prosperity and order, where a city was hardly to exist, and the myth of the resuscitating American Western Garden of the World, as Henry Nash Smith has described it in *Virgin Land*.[10] On a larger scale, Charlemont also is Simms's metaphor for all the unrealized hopes of humanity for peaceful material and spiritual fulfillment in the tragic cycle of life, endeavor, loss, and death that has existed since the Fall. In no other of his romances does Simms state his pastoral dilemma so succinctly as in *Charlemont:* that troubled urge toward Doing balanced by a simultaneous desire for an idyllic, calm stasis that just cannot be maintained. In this frequently labored romance of action gone wrong—in the ambition of Margaret Cooper to be a great poet, and of her village neighbors to have something better than rural peace in their lives—Simms at his most pessimistic writes that "it is man's terrible commission to destroy" in a world that "is a sort of

10. Henry Nash Smith, *Virgin Land: The American West as Symbol and Myth* (Cambridge, Mass., 1970), 12, 123–24, 188, 253–56.

vast moral lazar-house in which most have sores, either of greater or less degree of virulence" (55, 276).

If a *locus amoenus* is lost in *Charlemont*, another seems to be gained in Simms's masterpiece *Woodcraft*, chronologically the last of the Revolutionary War romances he wrote with the idea of showing the rest of the nation the important part played by the South in winning the fight for American independence. First titled *The Sword and the Distaff; or, Fair, Fat and Forty,* the romance *Woodcraft; or, Hawks about the Dovecote* tells of Captain Porgy's return from service with Francis Marion's partisans to his ruined South Carolina plantation Glen-Eberley. Riding with him through a dismal, impoverished countryside are his friends and wartime companions Sergeant Millhouse, young Ensign Lance Frampton, and Porgy's slave Tom. Later Glen-Eberley is almost lost to the mortgage-holding villain M'Kewn, who is the obligatory threatening counterforce from outside the idyllic place. The practical Millhouse and the self-sufficient, genially independent Widow Eveleigh—another of Simms's memorable female creations—help Porgy defeat M'Kewn and restore Glen-Eberley's land to productivity. Earlier, settled back into his sacked plantation with its frightened slaves, easygoing, reclusive Porgy takes on a resemblance to Meliboeus of Virgil's First Eclogue because he will not adjust to pressing realities outside his pastoral place. Widow Eveleigh in her fashion resembles Virgil's other farmer, the wise Tityrus, who makes adjustments to survive. During the war, for example, to keep her plantation she had made certain unsavory concessions to the nonbucolic world, such as trading sharply with the British enemy even though patriots looked down on such commerce. It is largely her determination that entraps M'Kewn.

As *Woodcraft* ends a mildly discontented, resigned Porgy retires from the worldly activity of paying his debts and courting, to live with his male companions on his prospering, isolated farm. Gentlemanly in manner, intellectual in discourse, noble in deed—fat, bibulous, comical, verbose, irresponsible Porgy is in part an Old South version of Falstaff and in part a self-portrait of Simms. Simms's first biographer William Peterfield Trent writes that he had it "on good authority" that

Simms identified himself with Porgy, although Trent does not reveal his source.[11] Appearing in all the Revolutionary War romances except *The Scout* (1841), the captain was so popular among Simms's readers that as early as 1836 Simms could tell James Lawson enthusiastically that Porgy "is actually the founder of a sect" of devoted followers (Simms, *Letters*, I, 82). In *The Dispossessed Garden* Lewis P. Simpson calls Porgy's retreat to Glen-Eberley a "confusing and sterile fulfillment."[12] But there is really nothing confusing and sterile about Porgy's rural bachelor retirement with his tried and true wartime friends if a reader sees in it a reflection of Simms's dislike, not for beneficial progress, but for the distracting and destructive physical restlessness of his America. In his fiction Simms deplored the misdirected, wasted activity of border robbers such as Guy Rivers, or the ruinous South Carolina civil war of the Revolutionary period that almost wrecked such idylls as Glen-Eberley, or the vain and wasted ambition of discontented and brilliant individuals such as Margaret Cooper.

It is possible to see in Porgy's withdrawal a reflection of Simms's own gently self-mocking pastoral urge to retire from his personal despair and everyday responsibilities at Woodlands and in Charleston—farming, writing, editing, managing slaves, rearing children, dining, bookkeeping, talking late over Madeira and pecans and advising and befriending younger southern authors such as Henry Timrod and John Esten Cooke. Like many thoughtful southerners of his time, Simms worried as well about the sectionalism that was isolating, frightening, and antagonizing the South in the 1840s and 1850s. In 1850 he wrote the New York editor Evert Augustus Duyckinck that "the national cauldron [is] bubbling up furiously, and about to boil over . . . to the great terror of the country, you may be certain" (Simms, *Letters*, III, 73). Thus, on one level the meaning of Glen-Eberley can be seen as a simple case of wish-fulfillment. In creating Porgy and his bachelor environ-

11. H. M. Jarrell, "Falstaff and Simms's Porgy," *American Literature*, III (May 1931), 204–12; Hugh W. Hetherington, *Cavalier of Old South Carolina: William Gilmore Simms's Captain Porgy* (Chapel Hill, 1966), 21–38; William Peterfield Trent, *William Gilmore Simms* (1892; rpr. New York, 1968), 109.

12. Simpson, *The Dispossessed Garden*, 60.

ment, Simms could withdraw vicariously from his everyday worries, fears, and overburdening activities. There is, in short, nothing confusing or sterile about Glen-Eberley if it is seen as an antebellum plantation version of Andrew Marvell's wonderfully cynical and humorous statement in praise of bachelorhood in "The Garden" that "Two Paradises 'twere in one / To live in Paradise alone."

More than anything else, however, Glen-Eberley represents Simms's compelling prognostication for the South. Like the Nashville Agrarians of the 1920s and 1930s, Simms felt that true prosperity and happiness for his area would result from agriculture. In an essay called "The Ages of Gold and Iron" that he wrote for the May 1841 *Ladies' Companion*, he calls farming a "divine institution." In *Woodcraft* Simms presents a picture of a tranquil, agricultural South from which foreign elements—namely, the British and their American allies—have been extirpated, and in which a racially harmonious community of planters, yeomen, and slaves has been established. He makes a point of showing how black Tom is as much Porgy's intimate friend as his servant, and one who is integral to the southern *locus amoenus*. Unlike Swallow Barn's Abe, Glen-Eberley's Tom remains in the pastoral place. Tom is a defender of the bucolic status quo—at least insofar as the Old South's peculiar institution is concerned—when he says to his master Porgy that he, Tom, speaks for all his fellow slaves in his rejection of the freedom Porgy has offered him: "You hab for keep dis nigger long as he lib; and him for keep you. . . . *You* b'longs to *me* Tom, jes' as much as me Tom b'long to *you;* and you nebber guine git *you* free paper from me long as you lib."[13] Simms wrote in a letter to Hammond at the end of 1852 that *Woodcraft* was "as good an answer" as any to Harriet Beecher Stowe's *Uncle Tom's Cabin* (Simms, *Letters*, III, 222–23).

But the issue of Glen-Eberley is essentially more compli-

---

13. William Gilmore Simms, "The Ages of Gold and Iron," *Ladies' Companion*, XV (May 1841), 12; William Gilmore Simms, [*Woodcraft.*] *The Sword and the Distaff* (Philadelphia, 1853), 580–81. All references to *Woodcraft* will be taken from this edition and noted parenthetically by page number in the text.

cated than even these explanations would have it be. Porgy is
a pastoral incompetent. When he courts a second widow, Mrs.
Griffin, after Widow Eveleigh has rejected him, preferring his
friendship to his love, he forgets the seriousness of the matter
he is about. Porgy thinks of himself as a pastoral swain. "Notions of arcadian felicity" creep into his mind, and "every
thing seemed perfect, and perfectly delightful about the hum-
ble cottage of the Widow Griffin. The trees had a fresher look;
the grounds seemed to shelter the most seductive recesses;
even the dog lying down on the piazza, and the cow ruminat-
ing under the old Pride of India before the door, seemed to enjoy dreams of a happier sort than usually come to dog and
cow in ordinary life. The skies above the cottage appeared to
wear looks of superior mildness and beauty" (422).

Everything is not perfect, though. The idyll is doomed.
Porgy is only deluding himself in his bucolic paradise. The
good Widow Griffin thinks he is ridiculous in his dreamy,
plump, incompetent attentions to her. He does not win her
hand, having lapsed as Simms says into "his arcadian mood,"
which makes him "obtuse in respect to the queer figure which
he cut in this novel employment"—great-bellied, vague-eyed,
in blue military coat and buff breeches Tom had to sew him
into, top-booted, his arms tangled in the yarn he is trying to
help her wind (587). Porgy's eyes are not on the worthy widow's, but rather rest on the invitingly green and softly shim-
mering landscape idyll beyond the shady piazza.

What *Woodcraft* finally amounts to is Simms's swan song
for his beloved agrarian Revolutionary War era in America.
In an authorial comment at the end of *Eutaw* Simms fixes
America's Golden Age in the Revolutionary era, when the na-
tion was unindustrialized and united against a common foe.[14]
That generation was gone, and so too was the Jeffersonian–
agrarian southern dream for a self-sufficient, rural United
States. Just as Charlemont is doomed, so is Glen-Eberley.
Each *locus amoenus* is a startling antebellum metaphor in
Simms's subtly critical pastoral for the troubled, threatened,

14. William Gilmore Simms, *Eutaw: A Tale of the Revolution* (New York,
1856), 582.

and ill-fated agricultural South of his day. If we can disagree over whether Porgy's retreat from the widows to Glen-Eberley is "confusing and sterile," we must nevertheless agree with Simpson's further statement in the same place that Porgy's plantation is, after all, "a world which has no future, for it has no female dimension . . . a world without issue doomed to come to an end."

Sergeant Millhouse speaks the last lines in the romance. Sitting, smoking, talking, and drinking by candlelight at the tankard-ringed table in the wainscoted dining room at Glen-Eberley, Porgy vows to devote the rest of his life to the company and comfort of his male friends. At his elbow Millhouse says, "The grapes is sour" (591). True enough also, perhaps, for Simms. Pessimism and despair are reflected in the junction of the ideal and the real that occurs in the pastoral imagery of Simms's long fiction. The contentment and serenity posited by all of his idylls are delusory. Like the ambitions of Guy Rivers and Margaret Cooper or the passing idyll of Charlemont, Glen-Eberley is a dream and a dead end. For Simms, the southern plantation is not an obtainable ideal. It is, rather, bitterly indicative of the vanity of human wishes. It is a chimera, a mere golden dream of self-contained and quiet rural contentment and prosperity in times that Simms knew only too well belonged to inevitable and destructive change.

7

John Esten Cooke and
Some Autumn Gossamer

As a young author and attorney gaining recognition socially and professionally in Richmond, Virginia, in the 1850s, John Esten Cooke regarded William Gilmore Simms as his good friend and literary master. Simms admired Cooke's fiction, poetry, and essays, but advised him to take more time in writing. Aware of the technical problems in his own work, Simms saw only too well that Cooke's rapidity of composition and dislike for revision were responsible for his most glaring weaknesses of style and plot (Simms, *Letters*, III, 355; IV, 115, 164–65, 180–81n, 215). Whatever their intrinsic literary quality, however, the number of well-received romances Cooke produced so enthusiastically if carelessly in the decade of the 1850s and in the five years between 1865 and 1870 led William Peterfield Trent to state that he was the South's most prominent romancer after Simms. In *Ante-bellum Southern Literary Critics*, Edd Winfield Parks places Cooke among only two others, Poe and Simms, who can be considered professional southern authors of their time.[1]

The tales Cooke published so quickly right after the Civil War contain remarkably little pastoral allusion of the kind that dominates as nostalgic imagery in his antebellum fiction. Furthermore, he was unwilling to treat his military experiences—first in the Confederate artillery and cavalry and finally on Jeb Stuart's staff—with the realistic detail and serious reflectiveness that John William De Forest, a veteran of the northern side, gave to his in *Miss Ravenel's Conversion from Secession to Loyalty*, published in 1867. In such senti-

1. Trent, *William Gilmore Simms*, 194; Edd Winfield Parks, *Ante-bellum Southern Literary Critics* (Athens, Ga., 1962), 66.

mental tales of the war as *Surry of Eagle's Nest* or *Mohun*, brought out in 1866 and 1869, respectively, Cooke's work is a disappointment compared to what he might have accomplished had he written with honest emotion and observation about the struggle from a southern participant's point of view. Like Simms, who kept trying to republish his antebellum romances until his death in 1870, Cooke refused to go along with the postwar turn to greater objectivity and realism in serious American fiction that was given such a boost by De Forest and promoted with lasting success by William Dean Howells. Cooke would not slow down his speed of composition or relinquish the high-flown diction, improbable adventure situations, and superficiality of characterization that for today's reader are the delight and bane of nineteenth-century romance. Of course, the mass market for which he wrote to earn his living expected this sort of thing.

It is hard not to agree with Jay B. Hubbell when he says that Cooke never became the writer he promised to be in his antebellum apprenticeship. Primarily because of their fresh, creative eagerness, I think, not to mention their promise, John Esten Cooke's best works remain the softly picturesque, often sweetly languid, always nostalgic youthful romances he wrote with Simms's encouragement and advice in a terrific burst of literary energy between 1853 and 1856. In the *Autobiographical Memo* he wrote for Simms in 1867, Cooke states that the best of these are, in his opinion and in this order: *The Virginia Comedians* (1854), initially a magazine serial; *Leather Stocking and Silk* (1854), his first romance in book form; and *The Youth of Jefferson* (1854), a pastoral confection based on a flirtation Jefferson is supposed to have had when he was a student at William and Mary in 1764.[2] Cooke makes the most of the irreverent, youthfully joyous interlude, turning the people and landscape of pre-Revolutionary Tidewater Virginia into an idyll that is almost entirely frivolous.

In the artificially sustained pastoral environment of *The Youth of Jefferson*, time for once is no enemy. Biographical and historical credibility are ignored, and it appears that the un-

2. Hubbell, *The South in American Literature*, 518, 520; John O. Beaty, *John Esten Cooke, Virginian* (1922; rpr. Port Washington, N.Y., 1965), 48.

dergraduate protagonists will never have to grow up. Called Sir Asinus, Jefferson innocently romps with his college friend "melancholy Jacques" through a cheerfully bucolic May Day countryside they like to imagine as the abode of "sylvan queens—dryads and naiads."[3] They pursue lady loves variously named Belinda, Amaryllis, Philippa, and Chloe, while imagining themselves as love-smitten Corydons or Pans who are in "Arcadia at last!" (242). Yet midway through the story Cooke pauses to justify his pastoral lark, posing a direct question to his readers to lead them to identify with his purpose. The melancholy tone of his reflection, yearning all of a sudden for something that is lost, provides an unexpected counterbalance to the lighthearted, lightheaded sense of bucolic play that pervades the romance. With a voice that recalls the wistful pastoral pauses where Simms intrudes his personal discontent with his times into the narrative flow of his fiction, Cooke appeals: "Have you never tried to fill your hearts with dreams, to close your vision to the present, and to bathe your weary forehead in those golden waters flowing from the dreamland of the past?" (127). For a moment in the happy idyllic stasis of *The Youth of Jefferson,* the ancient pastoral dichotomy casts the shadow of its dark, critical edge of dissatisfaction with the present.

Of all the frontiersman-hunter figures of antebellum romance only old John Myers of *Leather Stocking and Silk* is a widower and retired from forest life. Of all the others only he does not regret the passage of time and the loss of his free outdoor ways. The romance opens in the year 1810, as young Maximilian Courtlandt expresses admiration for the independent, rugged forest life Myers once was able to lead far away from the influence of towns. Myers is amused to hear this. Living out a comfortable old age dressed in decorative buckskins and homespun at Martinsburg—at the time of their conversation a quiet mountain-protected town in the valley of Virginia—he responds in an unusual way for a Cooke char-

---

3. John Esten Cooke, *The Youth of Jefferson; or, A Chronicle of College Scrapes at Williamsburg in Virginia, A. D. 1764* (New York, 1854), 63–65. All references to the work will be taken from this edition and noted parenthetically by page number in the text.

acter. Myers disparages the past. "They were hard times," he says to Max, "and I never want to see 'em back."[4] He is talking before the railroad's arrival in Martinsburg.

Underneath the "kindly atmosphere," as Beaty calls it, and many happily resolved courtships of *Leather Stocking and Silk* runs a nagging worry about social and economic change in America brought about by the proliferation of steam-powered machines.[5] Like Paulding, Kennedy, Hawthorne, Thoreau, Caruthers, and, in his ambivalent way, Simms, Cooke questioned the degrading effects on humanity of advances in technology. The machine that intrudes into his valley of Virginia Eden at mid-century is disquieting and dehumanizing in the extreme. Hunter John Myers's retirement is peaceful in the first decade of the nineteenth century, but the times are out of joint for his successors as the century wears to the end of its first fifty years—and Cooke in fiction comments caustically upon what he sees. *Leather Stocking and Silk*, in short, provides Cooke, as an antebellum southern social critic, a vehicle for serious pastoral complaint against the "cold prosaic hand" of "modern innovation" (395), represented by a steam locomotive that regularly roars through Martinsburg. Cooke's image has the same startling, disconcerting impact as James Kirke Paulding's Isle of Machines in *Letters from the South*.

Before the reader is introduced to contented John Myers living in a tranquil, bucolic Martinsburg as it was in an earlier decade, Cooke pictures the town at mid-century. By then, its everyday activities are punctuated by an unnatural, mechanical scream that literally controls the responses of the townspeople. Martinsburg "is now a busy, bustling town," he writes, "which daily raises its two thousand heads and hushes its two thousand tongues to listen to the shrill steam whistle of the cars." Employing the usual system of pastoral counterbalances, in the very next line Cooke moves away from the less idyllic present and goes back in his narrative to the time of Hunter John, when Martinsburg enjoyed a rural "thought-

4. Cooke, *Leather Stocking and Silk*, 35. All references to the work will be taken from this edition and noted parenthetically by page number in the text.

5. Beaty, *John Esten Cooke*, 36.

ful, slumbrous quietude" that is now "so completely a thing of the past" (7–8). Max Courtlandt later pronounces Cooke's recurring nostalgic philosophy that bygone times were better because they were more idyllically tranquil, as he perceived them, than the troubled present. Cooke has Courtlandt comment: "The present is not equal to the bright past in anything" (300).

Time, the great enemy in pastoral, is symbolized in *Leather Stocking and Silk* by a rush of wood and iron railroad cars, an image of disjuncture and threat that brackets the romance as the hawk brackets John Davis's *First Settlers of Virginia*. Near the conclusion of his story Cooke refers to the railroad again when he comments with unhappy resignation that "the cars had come, arousing with their shrill scream the long dormant echoes of the quiet countryside" (244). Max speaks for him once more when he muses on change at mid-century in an appropriate end-of-cycle autumn season: "Now who could have imagined that this beautiful and well-proportioned nature would change . . . but all things change . . . all these leaves so gayly dancing in the wind will soon be gone . . . they grow old and change" (269).

In the pre-Revolutionary rural Virginia setting of *The Virginia Comedians* Cooke's moody protagonist, Champ Effingham, is a restless residual spirit of Old World social oppression who has been corrupted by his European grand tour. He affects the haughty manners and malaise of a London rake at his father's Tidewater mansion Effingham Hall. The critical perspective opened up by the jaded character of Champ is directed against the un-American, un-Jeffersonian values of European class systems. As a would-be aristocrat in the southern garden, malcontented Champ first appears as a disruptive sojourner in the pastoral place. At the theater in Williamsburg he tries to seduce the British actress Beatrice Hallam. She rebuffs him publicly. After Champ kidnaps her, Beatrice's American beau Charles Waters comes to her rescue. He is Cooke's spokesman in this romance for democratic social and political reform. Thinking he has killed Charles, Champ flees to England. When Waters recovers, he marries Beatrice and they withdraw embittered to the mountains where she dies of fever.

The social privilege that works to protect young Effingham destroys these lovers. Eventually Champ returns to Virginia from abroad a second time, but he is cowed now and lives in self-imposed seclusion at Effingham Hall.

Slowly the bucolic environment to which Champ has returned works its magic. In the country the "healthful voice of nature" speaks to "his heart," and his spiritual calm is restored.[6] Earlier, when Beatrice Hallam arrived from London in colonial Virginia with a troupe of traveling players from which the romance takes its title, she adapted easily and joyfully to the New World's forests, fields, and waters, while the citified, alienated Champ Effingham, also fresh from London, brooded discontentedly in his father's house. Beatrice is the sojourner who is restored by the *locus amoenus,* the Virginia garden of the world. Her spirit is freed by her first encounter with rural America, where Charles Waters feels humankind will also find political regeneration (I, 134). Cooke describes the transformed Beatrice as a "pure child of the wilderness in spite of the eternal claims which an artificial civilization" have made upon her. "She rejoiced in the forests, and in the hills." Sailing with Charles on the James River "she was free as the bright water." Rejuvenated in the outdoors she becomes happy and carefree as a child again. While describing these idyllic events Cooke comments in his own voice on how good it is for individuals to get away from the bustling, eternally striving city and the responsibilities of study and business (I, 80–83).

But true to the pastoral pattern that evolves in antebellum southern romance, idyllic peace does not last for long in *The Virginia Comedians,* and it is not portrayed as an obtainable ideal. Furthermore, the bucolic contentment of Beatrice and Charles is threatened by approaching revolution, a far greater problem for these protagonists than the local infractions of Champ Effingham. Essentially, *The Virginia Comedians* is a strangely melancholy tale of unhappy love, exile, and death

---

6. John Esten Cooke, *The Virginia Comedians; or, Old Days in the Old Dominion* (2 vols. in 1; New York, 1883), II,155. All references to the work will be taken from this edition and noted parenthetically by volume and page number in the text.

where passing bucolic calms are disturbed by an outside world whose growing divisional political turmoil is an apposite reflection of Cooke's troubled decade of the 1850s. Between pastoral interludes with Beatrice, Charles Waters is lectured in revolutionary politics by a mysterious man in a red cloak. This character is a greatly exaggerated portrayal of Patrick Henry, who recalls Simms's furiously demented Guy Rivers more than the historical Henry, whatever his faults might have been.

The quality Cooke attacks in his melodramatic, unsavory representation of Patrick Henry is the demagogy of unthinking, time-serving politicians who were stirring divisive and demeaning abolition and secession sentiment in the North and South of his own day. Henry's irresponsible political agitation pictured in *The Virginia Comedians* is a perversion, in Cooke's view, of the levelheaded political processes Charles Waters wants to have instituted in the freed colonies. Henry gloats over the social and political decay of the Old World and over visions of future wars and rampaging mobs in England, Europe, and in the New World as well (I, 189–95). Needless to say, Cooke certainly did not object to America's breaking away from Britain, or to the war that had to be fought to accomplish this. Henry's intent is not at issue here, but rather his method. As his own era seemed to be facing another national crisis of rebellion and war, Cooke worriedly ends his romance on a note of gloomy foreboding. Strife and discord are fomented by the overheated goadings of men like Henry. In view of his high status in the pantheon of American Revolutionary heroes, Henry here becomes a powerful and unusual metaphor of the dark, destructive movements of time and change.

Cooke applies his urban gothic special effects with a heavy hand in the last pages of *The Virginia Comedians*. Nature's frame is no longer idyllic and amiable as it was at the start of the romance when Beatrice and Charles sailed, hiked, and hoped. Storm clouds gather and lightning crackles over Williamsburg as satanic Patrick Henry stands in the background goading a crazed anti-British rabble-rouser to even greater excesses of demagogic rhetoric as he addresses a mob of angry

colonials who are incensed over the Stamp Act. Stamps are
burned in the town square as a church bell tolls and lightning
flashes. With wild eyes and bleeding, foaming mouth the agi-
tator collapses exhausted into Henry's arms as the latter happily foresees the coming war of rebellion. In its gothic extrav-
agance this concluding scene is almost comic, except for what
it portends of social upheaval and war in Cooke's own time,
and for its message of the pernicious work of demagogues (II,
273–79).

As both William E. Walker and Mary Jo Jackson Bratton
demonstrate in their exhaustive studies of Cooke's life and
writings, there is no evidence that he supported the idea of
southern separation from the Union advocated in the mid-
1850s by his friend William Gilmore Simms and such hot-
heads as his fellow Virginian Edmund Ruffin. Cooke accepted
secession only after the firing on Fort Sumter, when Lincoln
called for troops from Virginia to help suppress rebellion else-
where in the South. This mobilization order, Cooke felt, was
an affront to the honor of his native state. Even though he dis-
liked the increasing central authority of Washington over the
sovereign states, Cooke had a greater dislike for the social and
political disharmony stirred in times of growing crisis by
shortsighted demagogues such as the Patrick Henry he depicts
in *The Virginia Comedians.* Cooke was especially appalled
by the prospect of internecine strife of the kind that occurred
between Tory and Patriot Americans in the Revolution, which
Simms described with lurid and heartbreaking detail in the
romances he published in the 1840s and 1850s that dealt with
the Revolutionary fight against British rule in South Carolina. Ironically, Cooke was destined to experience this himself
as he served in Lee's Army of Northern Virginia while his
elder brother Philip St. George fought for the Union. But before the war began and he made his choice of sides, John
Esten Cooke wanted Virginia to remain part of the Union and
to play the dominant role it had taken in national politics in
the eighteenth and early nineteenth centuries.[7] In keeping

7. William E. Walker, "John Esten Cooke: A Critical Biography" (Ph.D.
dissertation, Vanderbilt University, 1957), 161, 373–83, 396–97; Mary Jo
Jackson Bratton, "John Esten Cooke: The Young Writer and the Old South"
(Ph.D. dissertation, University of North Carolina, 1969), 191–201, 288.

with this preference for national unity and peace, Cooke's theme in *The Last of the Foresters* is the need to accept change in an often uncongenial and even unfamiliar world.

The story of a young man's coming of age and fitting into the larger community around him, *The Last of the Foresters* (1856) is a gentle extended allegory for Cooke's region. This neglected, seemingly inconsequential romance—like Simms's *Woodcraft* and Kennedy's *Swallow Barn* my favorite of the lot, and the most latently political of all—sets a daring example of the course the recalcitrant sovereign southern states must take, like it or not. Beneath its gossamer veil of pastoral autumn dalliances, allusions, and yearnings for something in life that is lost, *The Last of the Foresters* provides a desperately sincere message for Cooke's state and section on the unavoidable historical imperatives of social, political, and economic adjustment to change. The romance is much more than the easily dismissed "innocent entertainment" that Cooke himself calls it in the preface to the first edition—a necessary dissimulation nonetheless in view of the eschatological enormity of his prescription for the South to fit in and adjust to the times. As inevitable as the passage from childhood to adulthood, the process of this cure will require crucial readjustments of attitude and practice for his region as it becomes an integral part of the nation.

Told from the standpoint of a youth's education, maturation, and identification with a different role in society in the final decade of the eighteenth century, *The Last of the Foresters* is to my knowledge the only Bildungsroman written by a romancer of the Old South. As a subtle teacher in survival for his region, Cooke describes the transition experienced by his last forester Verty as he gives up his carefree, irresponsible old ways in the forest for new and burdensome values and concerns in the town. He must pass into another phase of his life as certainly and as irrevocably as the eighteenth century in which he was born is on the verge of passing into the nineteenth. After cavalierly dismissing the book's significance, Cooke goes on to say in his preface that he wrote his *fin-de-siècle* romance to show how the "wild nature" of a "young hunter—a child of the woods—was impressed by the new life and advancing civilization around him. The process of his mental development is the chief aim of the book." There is no nostalgia in this straightforward statement of intent. Verty simply must grow up and adjust to different ways. Pastoral—to use Andrew V. Ettin's succinct and apposite phraseology—"thrives on implications; it dwells amid nuances and flourishes in the shade."[8] For all the gentle, almost decadent qualities of its outdoor descriptions, *The Last of the Foresters*, especially in the severity of the local criticism its idyllic surfaces work to disguise, is a fitting capstone for this study of pastoral in antebellum southern romance.

Identified in the title as being at the end of his line as a type of character in southern romance, the glamorous, fey Verty has been softened and beautified into someone who resembles an artfully tousled Renaissance page in leather tights more than the traditionally rugged frontiersman-guide in rough buckskins. Verty is an uncertain seeker in the *locus amoenus*, responding with hesitation and wonder, but ultimately willing to go along with the forces of change at work both inside and outside of him. Nevertheless, unlike so many of his predecessors in southern fiction—with the notable exceptions of John Myers and Horse-Shoe Robinson—Verty, the last of the foresters, will not be defeated by society and progress. He will be transformed and absorbed by them, although he will not lose his identification with his locality in the nation. Cooke is careful to point this out at the end of his story.

Riding out of the Blue Ridge Mountains where he lives in a rustic lodge with an old Delaware squaw he calls "ma mere," pagelike Verty is first seen going toward Winchester, Cooke's boyhood home, to visit his sweetheart Redbud Summers. Cooke describes his *fin-de-siècle* hunter as a

> young man of about eighteen, mounted on a small, shaggy-coated horse, and clad in a wild forest costume, which defines clearly the outline of a person, slender, vigorous, and graceful. Over his brown forehead and smiling face, droops a wide hat, of soft white fur, below which, a mass of dark chestnut hair nearly covers his shoulders with its exuberant and tangled curls. . . . Verty carries in one hand a strange weapon, nothing less than a long cedar bow, and a

8. Ettin, *Literature and the Pastoral*, 96.

sheaf of arrows; in the other which also holds his rein, the antlers of a stag, huge and branching in all directions; around him circle two noble deer hounds.[9]

Shortly afterwards, sitting under a tree like a tapestry figure on sun-dappled grass, Verty tells Redbud he enjoys listening to her songs and lessons more than hunting. A hawk appears circling overhead as they talk. It has the same significance of inevitability as Davis's hawk that flies with Captain Argall's ship over the James River in *The First Settlers of Virginia*. Redbud asks Verty about his birth. Unknown to either, at the age of two he had been kidnapped by Delaware Indians in a raid upon his parents' settlement during which his real mother was killed. Reared by the Indians, Verty erroneously believes that "ma mere" is his mother. After Redbud has asked her question, Verty wants to shoot down the hawk with his bow and arrow, but she will not allow him to do this (14–15). As again symbolized by a hawk and Redbud's gesture, another world to which they must adjust is closing in on their idyll. After all, Cooke interjects nostalgically at a later point, carefree youth is an "elysian time which cannot last for any of us" (290).

Attorney Rushton, who turns out to be Verty's father, calls Cooke's last forester a "dream . . . a myth . . . a chimera" (351). As pastoral frontiersman-swain, a unique role for the hunter in antebellum romance, Verty is likened to a Strephon or a Corydon "taken back to Arcady" as he courts Redbud Summers in a fall season of gossamer hues, smoke and mist. Cooke likens her to a Chloe or Phillis, "some fair Daphne . . . fair shepherdess of Arcady" (68, 138, 232). In the gentle twilight of their adolescence, Verty and Redbud with their friends court, picnic, and stroll through the silken light and brittle colors of autumn. They fly kites in a beautiful "enchanting dream" whose "noble autumn forests moved away in magic splendor—red, and blue, and golden" (192, 225). Their transient, youthful activities are marked by the heavy, irrevocable

9. John Esten Cooke, *The Last of the Foresters; or, Humors on the Border: A Story of the Old Virginia Frontier* (New York, 1856), 12. All references to the work will be taken from this edition and noted parenthetically by page number in the text.

ticking of an old clock in the hall of Squire Summers's mansion at Apple Orchard Farm (10, 265, 311, 385). This recurring
image measures the minutes in the romance of the young
people's metaphorical journey toward integration into the
adult, urbanized community moving in other directions on
the borders of their idyll.

Back in the mountain lodge mellow with golden afternoon
sunlight a few weeks after he sat with Redbud while the hawk
flew overhead, Verty is asked by "ma mere" why he wants to
find out who he is, despite her assurances that she is his
mother. He answers with unexpected understanding and acceptance of what is happening to him as he is about to lose his
circumscribed boyhood Eden in the valley of Virginia. For
once in the romance Verty does not appear dreamy or sound
hesitant. Surprising too is the dignified ring of welcome ex-
pectation of change in his voice, on the edge of having to accept a new and more certain role in his life:

> Because the winds are changed and sing new songs; the leaves
> whisper as I pass, in a new voice; and even the clouds are not what
> they were to me when I ran after the shadows floating along the
> hills, and across the hollows. I have changed, *ma mere*, and the
> streams talk no more with the same tongue. I hear the flags and
> water-lilies muttering as I pass, and the world opens on me with a
> new strange light . . . I am not what I was. The world is open now
> and I must be a part of it. (365–66)

Verty does manage to make something of a fool of himself
along the way toward maturity and integration into his community when he tries to force change too quickly, unnecessar-
ily, and on bad advice. Visiting Redbud one day he is dressed
in a plum-colored "cavalier's suit," with ruffled shirt, knee
breeches, red heeled shoes, and a scarlet ribbon in his freshly
queued hair. He is uncomfortable in city clothes, and Redbud
is not favorably impressed by his foppish appearance. When
he puts on his more democratic and useful hunting leathers
again, she is pleased and feels "carried back to the old days"
(99, 119, 208). Cooke's point in this episode is to show that
Verty does not have to give up all that is natural to him of his
old identify as he passes into another phase of life. There is

room for continuity even in transition. Earlier in the romance Cooke indulged in typical pastoral protest against Yankee money grubbing, the "glorious race for cash" that is a corruption of progress because it debases human values. His complaint furnishes instruction in what to avoid: "The golden age of Arcady is gone so long—the new age has come! The crooks that wreathed round with flowers are changed into telegraph posts, and Corydon is on a three-legged stool busy with ledgers" (161). Verty will not be reduced quite to this, however, as he gives up his innocent forest ways to read law and study Latin and Greek in Rushton's office after his sessions with Redbud. He will keep his rural connections at Apple Orchard Farm after he marries her, and at his lodge in the nearby mountains.

Given the usual pattern of idyllic and nonidyllic juxtapositions in pastoral within the romance form of antebellum southern fiction, it is structurally appropriate and nostalgically apt for Cooke to have idyllic, dreamy Verty discover his true identity and place in the nonidyllic urbanized world to which he must adhere for survival while an annual saint's-day riot between German and Irish settlers is going on in the Winchester streets outside Rushton's dusty, cluttered office. By means of the engraved initials "A. R." on the clasp of a coral necklace Redbud wears, the gruff attorney makes the identification of his lost son. Somehow Verty had kept the necklace in his possession until an itinerant Jewish peddler stole it from the lodge and sold it in town. When Rushton discovers the source of Redbud's purchase, he gets the peddler to confess his theft. The mystery of Verty's parentage is solved, and his identity as Arthur Rushton is made as an urban riot crashes through the streets outdoors. So, amid sounds of an incomprehensible but determined struggling, Verty the chimerical boy-hunter becomes the adult Arthur, the lawyer's son and last of the foresters who is to wed Redbud Summers and take his place in the nonpastoral, workaday, often confusing community on the periphery of the *locus amoenus*— "breaking himself into the traces" as an attorney in town (298), leaving behind "that strange wild dream of the far past" (419).

The Last of the Foresters is a pastoral of acceptance and reconciliation, mutability and growing up—but not of complete
surrender to change. The romance ends with a description of
Verty's nostalgic return to his deserted lodge with one of his
old hunting dogs, Longears. This is the bucolic place of his
southern identification, despite his necessary adaptation to
the pressing world outside. The story is an object lesson for
Cooke's increasingly isolated and bedeviled region. The su-
premacy of old landed values in a traditional, rural society
was breaking down in America at the beginning of the second
half of the nineteenth century in the face of new, dimly understood and threatening forces of mechanization, industrialization, and immigration. As a result, certain national adjustments, like Verty's metaphorical personal one, had to be made
to different ways in an active, unromantic, and often contra-
dictory world.

The Last of the Foresters is a pastorally veiled appeal to the
South to fit in with changing times. Its covert argument for
national reconciliation is similar to the obvious one made in
The Kentuckian in New York, only Cooke is more unrelenting
thematically than is William Alexander Caruthers. Cooke sees
his argument through, for there is no pastoral withdrawal
from the world at the end of his tale as there is in Caruthers's.
As holds true for the outdoor adventure romances of the other
gentlemen-authors of the Old South, the underside of Cooke's
unique romance of growing up has its sharp, critical perspective on times that were falling apart. In view of the lateness of
the historical hour of sectional crisis at which his antebellum
romance appeared, however, *The Last of the Foresters* is imbued with the most urgent and surprising lesson of them all.

Bibliography

THE ROMANCES

Caruthers, William Alexander. *The Kentuckian in New York; or, The Adventures of Three Southerners.* 1834; rpr. Ridgewood, N.J., 1968.
——. *The Knights of the Golden Horse-Shoe: A Traditionary Tale of the Cocked Hat Gentry.* 1845; rpr. with introduction by C. C. Davis. Chapel Hill, N.C., 1970.

Cooke, John Esten. *The Last of the Foresters; or, Humors on the Border: A Story of the Old Virginia Frontier.* New York, 1856.
——. *Leather Stocking and Silk; or, Hunter John Myers and His Times. A Story of Virginia.* New York, 1854.
——. *Mohun; or, The Last Days of Lee and His Paladins.* New York, 1869.
——. *Surry of Eagle's Nest; or, The Memoirs of a Staff Officer Serving in Virginia.* New York, 1866.
——. *The Virginia Comedians; or, Old Days in the Old Dominion.* 2 vols. in 1. New York, 1883.
——. *The Youth of Jefferson; or, A Chronicle of College Scrapes at Williamsburg, in Virginia, A. D. 1764.* New York, 1854.

Davis, John. *The First Settlers of Virginia: An Historical Novel Exhibiting a View of the Rise and Progress of the Colony at James Town, a Picture of Indian Manners, the Countenance of the Country, and Its Natural Productions.* New York, 1806.

Holmes, Isaac E. *Recreations of George Taletell, F. Y. C.* Charleston, 1822.

Kennedy, John Pendleton. *Horse-Shoe Robinson: A Tale of the Tory Ascendency.* 1852; rpr. edited by Ernest E. Leisy. New York, 1937.
——. *Swallow Barn; or, A Sojourn in the Old Dominion.* 2 vols. Philadelphia, 1832.
——. *Swallow Barn; or, A Sojourn in the Old Dominion.* 1853; rpr. with introduction by W. S. Osborne. New York, 1962.

Paulding, James Kirke. *Letters from the South.* 2 vols. New York, 1835.
———. *Westward Ho! A Tale.* 2 vols. New York, 1832.
Ruffner, Reverend Dr. Henry. "Judith Bensaddi: A Tale." *Southern Literary Messenger,* V (July 1839), 469–505.
———. "Seclusaval; or, The Sequel to the Tale of 'Judith Bensaddi.'" *Southern Literary Messenger,* V (October 1839), 638–62.
Simms, William Gilmore. *Beauchampe; or, The Kentucky Tragedy. A Tale of Passion.* 2 vols. Philadelphia, 1842.
———. *Beauchampe; or, The Kentucky Tragedy.* 1856; rpr. Chicago, 1890.
———. *Charlemont; or, The Pride of the Village.* New York, 1856.
———. *Eutaw: A Tale of the Revolution.* New York, 1856.
———. *The Forayers; or, The Raid of the Dog-Days.* New York, 1855.
———. *Guy Rivers: A Tale of Georgia.* 2 vols. New York, 1834.
———. *Guy Rivers: A Tale of Georgia.* 1855; rpr. New York, 1882.
———. *Mellichampe: A Legend of the Santee.* 2 vols. New York, 1836.
———. *The Partisan: A Tale of the Revolution.* 2 vols. New York, 1835.
———. *The Scout; or, Black Riders of Congaree.* New York, 1854.
———. [*Woodcraft.*] *The Sword and the Distaff.* Philadelphia, 1853.

OTHER SOURCES

Alvord, Clarence W., and Lee Bidgood, eds. *The First Explorations of the Trans-Allegheny Region by the Virginians, 1650–1674.* Cleveland, 1912.
Baritz, Loren. *City on a Hill: A History of Ideas and Myths in America.* New York, 1964.
Bartram, William. *Travels Through North and South Carolina, Georgia, East and West Florida.* Edited by Mark Van Doren. New York, 1928.
Beaty, John O. *John Esten Cooke, Virginian.* 1922; rpr. Port Washington, N.Y., 1965.
Beverley, Robert. *The History and Present State of Virginia.* Edited by Louis B. Wright. Chapel Hill, 1947.
Bohner, Charles H. *John Pendleton Kennedy: Gentleman from Baltimore.* Baltimore, 1961.
Boorstin, Daniel J. *The Lost World of Thomas Jefferson.* New York, 1948.
Bradford, William. *Of Plymouth Plantation, 1620–1647.* Edited by Samuel Eliot Morison. New York, 1952.
Bratton, Mary Jo Jackson. "John Esten Cooke: The Young Writer and the Old South, 1831–1861." Ph.D. dissertation, University of North Carolina, 1969.

Cardwell, Guy A. "The Plantation House: An Analogical Image." *Southern Literary Journal*, II (Fall 1969), 3–21.

Cash, W. J. *The Mind of the South*. New York, 1954.

Chase, Richard. *The American Novel and Its Tradition*. New York, 1957.

Cirillo, Albert R. "*As You Like It*: Pastoralism Gone Awry." *Journal of English Literary History*, XXXVIII (1971), 19–39.

Congleton, J. E. *Theories of Pastoral Poetry in England, 1684–1798*. Gainesville, 1952.

Cooke, John Esten. *John Esten Cooke's Autobiographical Memo*. Edited by John R. Welsh. University of South Carolina Bibliographical Series No. 4, Columbia, 1969.

———. *Virginia: A History of the People*. Boston, 1884.

Cooper, James Fenimore. *The Pioneers; or, The Sources of the Susquehana. A Descriptive Tale*. 2 vols. New York, 1823.

———. *The Prairie: A Tale*. Introduction by H. N. Smith. New York, 1959.

Cowie, Alexander. *The Rise of the American Novel*. New York, 1948.

Craven, Avery O. *The Growth of Southern Nationalism, 1848–1861*. Baton Rouge, 1953.

Cullen, Patrick. *Spenser, Marvell, and Renaissance Pastoral*. Cambridge, Mass., 1970.

Davis, Curtis Carroll. *Chronicler of the Cavaliers: A Life of the Virginia Novelist Dr. William A. Caruthers*. Richmond, 1953.

———. "'Judith Bensaddi' and the Reverend Doctor Henry Ruffner." *Publications of the American Jewish Historical Society*, XXXIX (September 1949–June 1950), 115–42.

De Forest, John William. *Miss Ravenel's Conversion from Secession to Loyalty*. New York, 1867.

Eaton, Clement. *Freedom of Thought in the Old South*. Durham, 1940.

———. *The Growth of Southern Civilization, 1790–1860*. New York, 1961.

———. *The Mind of the Old South*. Baton Rouge, 1967.

Empson, William. *Some Versions of Pastoral*. Hammondsworth, 1966.

Ettin, Andrew V. *Literature and the Pastoral*. New Haven, 1984.

Faust, Drew Gilpin. *A Sacred Circle: The Dilemma of the Intellectual in the Old South, 1840–1860*. Baltimore, 1977.

Fitzgerald, F. Scott. *The Great Gatsby*. New York, 1953.

Force, Peter, ed. *Tracts and Other Papers, Relating Principally to the Origin, Settlement, and Progress of the Colonies in North America*. 4 vols. New York, 1947.

Forster, E. M. *Aspects of the Novel*. New York, 1927.

Frye, Northrop. *Anatomy of Criticism: Four Essays.* Princeton, N.J., 1957.

Gaines, Francis Pendleton. *The Southern Plantation: A Study in the Development and the Accuracy of a Tradition.* New York, 1925.

Gerber, Gerald E. "James Kirke Paulding and the Image of the Machine." *American Quarterly,* XXII (Fall 1970), 736–41.

Greg, Walter W. *Pastoral Poetry and Pastoral Drama.* New York, 1959.

Gwathmey, Edward M. *John Pendleton Kennedy.* New York, 1931.

Hakluyt, Richard. *The Principal Navigations.* 12 vols. New York, 1965.

Hawthorne, Nathaniel. *The American Notebooks.* Edited by Randall Stewart. New Haven, 1933.

———. *The Blithedale Romance.* 1852; rpr. with introduction by Arlin Turner. New York, 1958.

Helper, Hinton R. *The Impending Crisis of the South: How to Meet It.* New York, 1860.

Herold, Amos L. *James Kirke Paulding: Versatile American.* 1926; rpr. New York, 1966.

Hetherington, Hugh W. *Cavalier of Old South Carolina: William Gilmore Simms's Captain Porgy.* Chapel Hill, 1966.

Holman, C. Hugh. *The Roots of Southern Writing.* Athens, Ga., 1972.

Hubbell, Jay B. *The South in American Literature, 1607–1900.* Durham, 1954.

Hundley, D. R. *Social Relations in Our Southern States.* New York, 1860.

I'll Take My Stand: The South and the Agrarian Tradition. By Twelve Southerners. Introduction by Louis D. Rubin, Jr. New York, 1962.

Inge, M. Thomas. *Agrarianism in American Literature.* New York, 1969.

Irving, Washington. *The Sketch Book of Geoffrey Crayon.* New York, 1848.

Jarrell, H. M. "Falstaff and Simms's Porgy." *American Literature,* III (May 1931), 204–12.

Jefferson, Thomas. *Notes on the State of Virginia.* Edited by William Peden. Chapel Hill, 1955.

———. *The Writings of Thomas Jefferson.* 20 vols. Edited by Andrew Lipscomb. Washington, D.C., 1903.

Kazin, Alfred. *An American Procession: The Major American Writers from 1830 to 1930—The Crucial Century.* New York, 1984.

Kelley, Mary. *Private Woman, Public Stage: Literary Domesticity in Nineteenth-Century America.* New York, 1984.

Kibler, James Everett, Jr. "The First Simms Letters: 'Letters from the West' (1826)." *Southern Literary Journal,* XIX (Spring 1987), 81–91.

La Budde, Kenneth J. "The Rural Earth: Sylvan Paradise." *American Quarterly*, X (Summer 1958), 142–53.

Lankford, John, ed. *Captain John Smith's America*. New York, 1967.

Lawrence, D. H. *Studies in Classic American Literature*. New York, 1951.

Leisy, Ernest E. *The American Historical Novel*. Norman, Okla., 1950.

Lerner, Laurence. *The Uses of Nostalgia: Studies in Pastoral Poetry*. New York, 1972.

Levin, Harry. *The Myth of the Golden Age in the Renaissance*. Bloomington, Ind., 1969.

Lewis, R. W. B. *The American Adam: Innocence, Tragedy, and Tradition in the Nineteenth Century*. Chicago, 1955.

MacKethan, Lucinda Hardwick. *The Dream of Arcady: Place and Time in Southern Literature*. Baton Rouge, 1980.

Magowan, Robin. "Fromentin and Jewett: Pastoral Narrative in the Nineteenth Century." *Comparative Literature*, XVI (1964), 331–37.

Marvell, Andrew. *Poems and Letters*. Edited by H. M. Margoliouth. Oxford, 1952.

Marx, Leo. *The Machine in the Garden: Technology and the Pastoral Ideal in America*. New York, 1964.

———. "Pastoralism in America." In *Ideology and Classic American Literature*, edited by Sacvan Bercovitch and Myra Jehlen. New York, 1986.

Melville, Herman. *Moby-Dick; or, The Whale*. Introduction by Newton Arvin. New York, 1959.

Milton, John. *Complete Poetry and Selected Prose*. Introduction by Cleanth Brooks. New York, 1950.

Nash, Roderick. *Wilderness and the American Mind*. New Haven, 1973.

Noble, David W. *The Eternal Adam and the New World Garden*. New York, 1968.

Panofsky, Erwin. "'Et in Arcadia Ego': Poussin and the Elegiac Tradition." In *Pastoral and Romance: Modern Essays in Criticism*, edited by Eleanor Terry Lincoln. Englewood Cliffs, N.J., 1969.

Parks, Edd Winfield. *Ante-Bellum Southern Literary Critics*. Athens, Ga., 1962.

Parrington, Vernon Louis. *The Romantic Revolution in America, 1800–1860*. New York, 1927.

Paulding, James Kirke. *The Backwoodsman: A Poem*. Philadelphia, 1818.

———. *The Letters of James Kirke Paulding*. Edited by Ralph M. Aderman. Madison, 1962.

Paulding, William L. *Literary Life of James K. Paulding*. New York, 1867.

Poe, Edgar Allan. *The Complete Works.* 16 vols. Edited by James A. Harrison. New York, 1902.

Poggioli, Renato. *The Oaten Flute.* Cambridge, Mass., 1975.

Purchas, Samuel. *Hakluytus Posthumus; or, Purchas His Pilgrims.* 20 vols. Glasgow, 1905.

Putnam, Michael C. *Virgil's Pastoral Art.* Princeton, 1970.

Quinn, Arthur Hobson. *American Fiction: An Historical and Critical Survey.* New York, 1964.

———. *Edgar Allan Poe: A Critical Biography.* New York, 1942.

Quinn, David Beers, ed. *The Roanoke Voyages, 1584–1590.* Hakluyt Society, Series II. London, 1955.

Ridgely, J. V. *John Pendleton Kennedy.* New York, 1966.

———. *Nineteenth Century Southern Literature.* Lexington, Ky., 1980.

Rosenmeyer, Thomas G. *The Green Cabinet: Theocritus and the European Pastoral Lyric.* Berkeley, 1969.

Rubin, Louis D., Jr. *William Elliott Shoots a Bear: Essays on the Southern Literary Imagination.* Baton Rouge, 1975.

———. *The Writer in the South.* Athens, Ga., 1972.

Rubin, Louis D., Jr., *et al.*, eds. *The History of Southern Literature.* Baton Rouge, 1985.

Sanford, Charles L. *The Quest for Paradise: Europe and the American Moral Imagination.* Urbana, Ill., 1961.

Savage, Henry, Jr. *Seeds of Time: The Background of Southern Thinking.* New York, 1959.

Shakespeare, William. *The Tempest.* Edited by Frank Kermode. Cambridge, Mass., 1958.

Simms, William Gilmore. "The Ages of Gold and Iron." *Ladies' Companion,* XV (May 1841), 12–14.

———. *Egeria; or, Voices of Thought and Counsel, for the Woods and Wayside.* Philadelphia, 1853.

———. "The Good Farmer." *Ladies' Companion,* XV (August 1841), 154–57.

———. *The Letters of William Gilmore Simms.* 5 vols. Edited by Mary C. Simms Oliphant, Alfred Taylor Odell, and T. C. Duncan Eaves. Introduction by Donald Davidson. Columbia, S.C., 1952–56.

———. "Southern Literature." *Magnolia,* III (February 1841), 69–74.

———. *Southward Ho! A Spell of Sunshine.* New York, 1854.

Simpson, Lewis P. *The Dispossessed Garden: Pastoral and History in Southern Literature.* Athens, Ga., 1975.

Smith, Henry Nash. *Virgin Land: The American West as Symbol and Myth.* Cambridge, Mass., 1970.

Smith, John. *A True Relation of Virginia.* Introduction by Charles Deane. Boston, 1866.

Spenser, Edmund. *The Complete Poetical Works.* Edited by R. E. Neil Dodge. Boston, 1936.

Squires, Michael. *The Pastoral Novel: Studies in George Eliot, Thomas Hardy, and D. H. Lawrence.* Charlottesville, 1974.

Stowe, Harriet Beecher. *Uncle Tom's Cabin; or, Life Among the Lowly.* 1852; rpr. edited by Kenneth S. Lynn. Cambridge, Mass., 1962.

Taylor, William R. *Cavalier and Yankee: The Old South and American National Character.* New York, 1961.

Theocritus. *The Idylls of Theokritus.* Translated by Barriss Mills. West Lafayette, Ind., 1963.

Thoreau, Henry David. *Walden and Other Writings.* Edited by Brooks Atkinson. New York, 1950.

Timrod, Henry. "Literature in the South." *Russell's Magazine,* V (August 1859), 385–95.

Trent, William Peterfield. *William Gilmore Simms.* 1892; rpr. New York, 1968.

Tuckerman, Henry T. *The Life of John Pendleton Kennedy.* New York, 1871.

Virgil. *The Eclogues.* Translated by C. S. Calverley. New York, 1960.
———. *The Works of Virgil.* Translated by John Dryden. London, 1961.

Walker, William E. "John Esten Cooke: A Critical Biography." Ph.D. dissertation, Vanderbilt University, 1957.

Wilbur, Richard. "The House of Poe." In *Anniversary Lectures.* Library of Congress, Washington, D.C., 1959.

Woodward, C. Vann. *The Burden of Southern History.* Baton Rouge, 1968.

Wright, Louis B. *The Colonial Search for a Southern Eden.* University, Ala., 1953.
———. *The Elizabethans' America.* London, 1965.
———, ed. *A Voyage to Virginia in 1609: Two Narratives.* Charlottesville, 1964.

Wyatt-Brown, Bertram. *Southern Honor: Ethics and Behavior in the Old South.* New York, 1982.

Index